CAMINO

LAUGHTER AND TEARS ALONG SPAIN'S 500-MILE CAMINO DE SANTIAGO

D1206123

BY JOHN H CLARK III

Publishing services provided by **Archangel Ink**

ISBN: 1942761554
ISBN-13: 978-1-942761-55-6

Dedication

This book is dedicated to seekers and adventurers everywhere, and especially to the millions of pilgrims all across the world who have made the journey along the wonderful Camino de Santiago. Buen Camino, y'all ...

Table of Contents

Introduction

It was probably the most frightening thing I've ever done. Going to Spain.

I remember being basically held captive for hours in a bedroom at my in-law's house, nervously chain-smoking a box of Marlboros prior to getting married when I was 19 years old. Had a large semiautomatic pistol pointed in my face once when I stumbled into a pizza restaurant robbery. Watching my oldest daughter being born was exciting but scary as hell, especially when one of the nurses yelled at me for getting in the way. Riding a 1,500-pound rodeo bull was pretty scary, the first time. Getting up in front of a college class to give a speech is nerve-wracking. Woke up one time in a Harris County Jail cell in downtown Houston, and had no idea where I was. Standing in the front of an empty junior high school classroom my first year as a teacher, imagining a couple dozen teenagers staring back at me the first day of school was absolutely terrifying.

But the idea of traveling overseas, being 5,000 miles or so away from home, was possibly the scariest time of all.

For most people, I imagine, going to Europe is a tremendously exciting thing. Not a lot of people get that opportunity, at least not where I come from. I spent the first

31 years of my life in Houston, Texas, never living more than 20 miles away from the little 1,100-square-foot house where I grew up in the Langwood subdivision, near the Cypress Fairbanks area, across the railroad tracks and the old Hempstead Highway from Spring Branch.

When I was a kid, my family never went anywhere, and I never really imagined a world outside my hometown. Even after I graduated from college in 1987 and got a job offer with a newspaper 150 miles away in Temple, I didn't want to go – "Temple? Where in the hell is Temple?" – until one of my professors at the University of Houston convinced me it would be a good career move.

So the whole idea of going to Spain was extremely exciting, and also scared me half to death.

Even after I bought the plane ticket, I tried several times to talk myself out of going. On the way to the airport, I even had to give myself little pep talks. "C'mon, it's not like you're going to prison or something."

For one thing, I'd only been on an airplane two or three times, and never for more than three hours. Didn't particularly enjoy it, either. Three hours seemed like forever. I remember walking through the New Orleans airport after my first flight on my 25th birthday, deaf as a post from clogged-up ears. For another thing, I've always been a major homebody. I had driven cross-country a couple of times, gone to the Canadian side of Niagara Falls and a couple Mexican border towns, but to Europe? By myself? Any time I traveled any distance from home, by the time I got where I was going, I was ready to turn around and go back. I could literally get homesick going to Dallas for the weekend.

So even though I fantasized for a long time about going to Europe some day, actually doing it was never really a consideration. Little more than some kind of very far-off dream. Pure fantasy. Along with being a non-traveler, I never had the money for such a thing. Who did? Nobody I ever knew. Vacation was driving to South Padre Island for a couple of days, or maybe a trip to San Antonio.

Then, I reconnected one day via the Internet with an old friend from high school who has lived and traveled all over the world. Conversations with her, combined with a growing midlife crisis, rekindled my European adventure fantasy, and eventually I discovered the Camino de Santiago pilgrimage in northern Spain. I did lots and lots of research, and found myself increasingly drawn to it. People talked about the spirituality of the place, the beauty, the self-discovery, the life-changing experiences.

So, off I went. And like always, it wasn't long after I got there that I wanted to turn around and come back home. I wanted to come back home in a big way. I even used the laptop computer in the hotel lobby in Pamplona shortly after I arrived to see how much it would cost me to buy a plane ticket and get the hell out of there. Fortunately, the price was outrageous. Unbeknownst to me, I probably could have just changed my initial reservation and come on back for a comparatively nominal fee, but I didn't know about such things at that time.

So I stayed. And I walked 500-plus miles across the country. And it was magical. Absolutely magical. The first three or four days were terrifying, but after I settled down and realized I wasn't going to die or something, it became one of the greatest months of my life.

I didn't take a telephone with me – which amazed some people – but I made use of various coin-operated computers all along the way for email communications back home, and also to chronicle everything in a blog. That blog is the basis of this book, along with additional commentary I added later. I met wonderful people along the way, from countries all over the world. We walked and talked and laughed and sang and suffered together. I've never felt more alive than during those days on the Camino. I hope you enjoy reading about it half as much as I enjoy telling about it.

June 9

A rainy night in Pamplona, and I'm standing under an awning alongside the famed Plaza del Castillo, soaking wet and smoking a nice cigar. All the bars and cafes around the Plaza are busy, and people are huddled out of the rain, drinking and eating and talking and laughing.

I arrived here only a few hours ago, and I'm wanting to ask someone if there is a store nearby, where I can buy some bread and meat for a sandwich, to take back to my hotel room. It's been a very long day of travel from the U.S., and I am tired. I'm a little shy about my Spanish, so I wait for a friendly face to walk by. I spot a likely suspect and say, "Senor?" He takes one look at me, bedraggled and drenched, wearing a pair of khaki cargo shorts, a blue pullover fleece shirt and worn flip-flop sandals, and says, "No, no, no," and starts to quickly walk away. Just as quickly, I move toward him and say, "Buscando para una tienda (I'm looking for a store)." He stops and we talk for just a second and then he says, "You speak English?" Could it have been the accent? I say, yes, and he directs me across the plaza and down a couple narrow streets to a little convenience store type shop, where I find what I want: a package of Spanish ham, some cheese and a small loaf of crusty bread. Oh, and two ice-cold cans of San Miguel.

Like I said, it was a hellish day of travel that got even worse when I landed in Madrid. Finding oneself in a foreign country, without being fluent in the language, is not as easy a proposition as it might seem. Asking the right questions is easy enough for me – I took Spanish in high school and actually minored in Spanish in college – but the problem comes in understanding the rapid-fire responses. It took what seemed forever to find the right bus to get me headed from the airport toward Pamplona, and by the time I finally managed to get from Barajas to the bus station in downtown Madrid, I was seriously freaking out. As I sat for several hours waiting for my bus, I kept thinking, over and over, "What in the hell have you done? What were you thinking?"

I finally made it to Pamplona, though, without much real incident, other than a gut-wrenching fear of being stranded forever in a foreign country. Needless to say, my mind gets a little carried away sometimes. And when I popped up out of the underground bus station, a Spanish angel happened to cross my path and rescue the day.

She was the second person I asked about the hotel where I had a reservation, if they knew where it was and could they direct me. Both the hotel and the bus station were supposed to be very near the Plaza del Castillo, so I thought that I would have no trouble getting where I needed to be. As I stood there on the sidewalk looking around, however, I had no clue which direction to go. Someone later told me that when one travels to an unfamiliar place, it is a good idea to carry some sort of map. Oh, yeah, ahem, um … good idea.

People were walking to and fro, so I approached a young man and asked if he knew of my hotel. He said, "No, no," and kept walking. When I asked the next person, a young lady, she smiled and said (in Spanish) that not only did she know the hotel, she was headed that way and would I like to walk with her? Boy, howdy, would I ever! She chatted incessantly and acted as a tour guide while we walked about 10 minutes to the hotel, which is indeed right off the Plaza. I didn't catch everything she said, but I understood quite a bit, and was mostly very grateful for her help. I must have looked pretty tired, because she even offered to carry my bag for me at one point. When we reached the front door of the hotel, she smiled and waved and walked away. I didn't catch her name, but I certainly said, "Muchas gracias."

———

Traveling to Spain was sort of a dream come true. A fantasy come to life, really. I've lived all my life in Texas, and never been overseas. Hell, growing up in Houston, we never went anywhere, and I had no real concept of life outside my own hometown. As I got older, I'd often wondered what it would be like to drop myself in the middle of Europe somewhere, just me and a backpack, and travel around. Ride the trains and just wander from place to place. You hear about people doing stuff like that, and it always sounded really exotic and cool and exciting.

Despite the fact that I have never particularly enjoyed traveling, haven't really been that many places, and usually start getting homesick a few days after I go pretty much anywhere out of town, this urge and curiosity grew stronger over the years. One day, I was messing around on the computer and did a search for "backpacking trips in Europe." One of the things that came up was the Camino de Santiago, a 750-kilometer pilgrimage across northern Spain that began 1,200 years ago. It sounded interesting, so I searched some more. I read everything I could find about the Camino, which in English translates as The Way of St. James, and something about it struck me. Took hold of me, and would not let go. Although I'd only been outside the United States three times – a childhood trip with my parents to some Texas-Mexico border town; going to Monterrey, Mexico with my teenage football team; and a visit with my wife, sister-in-law and brother-in-law to the Canadian side of Niagara Falls – I decided this was something I very much wanted to do. Needed to do. Fly 5,000 miles to the other side of the world with nothing but a backpack, and walk by myself 400-plus miles across a foreign country. I had to do it.

I felt at that time like life was passing me by. I was 53 years old, and had never really done anything big. Never had big adventures. No major accomplishments, to speak of. Nothing really outstanding, at least not to me. Sure, I went to college and got my degree. Had a house and a wife and kids, a successful career in journalism, and was now working as a public school teacher. That sounds like a pretty successful life, by many definitions. But I knew better. I had wasted a lot of time in my younger days; wasted a lot of years. Squandered so many talents. Made so many mistakes and bad decisions. Blew so many opportunities. Fell short in so many ways.

People I grew up with and went to school with and played sports with had done so many amazing things. One kid who grew up a few blocks from me started his own company and became a millionaire. Another guy was star quarterback on his high school and college football teams, won a state championship, a national championship and is in his university's Hall of Fame. Another played big-time college basketball and became a successful major college coach. Others were doctors, lawyers, had lived in foreign countries and traveled the world. Hmm, traveled the world. Maybe I could at least do that.

So, I read and researched and read some more over the next few months, joined an Internet chat forum about the Camino, bought my plane tickets, started planning and buying equipment – hiking shoes, hiking socks, backpack, etc. – training on the weekends, doing more research. I was more and more nervous about it as the trip got closer and closer, but I thought I was pretty well prepared.

The big day finally came, two days after school closed for summer break, and I was nervous as hell. I told myself, hey, c'mon, it's not like you're going to prison or something. And off I went. The first two legs of my flights were fairly smooth. I flew to Dallas, found my way OK around that monstrosity of an airport, and then flew on to Newark, New Jersey, where I had a short layover before my connection to Madrid. The layover was something like two hours, so I wandered through the airport terminal to kill some time and find something to eat. When I headed back to my gate, I saw people lined up to board a flight. I showed a guy standing at the back of the line my boarding pass and asked him which flight this was, and he pointed at my pass and said, "This one." Good grief, I'd forgotten to reset my watch and nearly missed the damn flight.

On the plane, I learned that the woman seated next to me was heading home to Madrid, from a vacation with a travel group to New York City. She spoke no English at all, so I decided this was a good opportunity to try out some of my Spanish. We talked quite a bit – sometimes successfully; sometimes not so much – but it was fun, and I asked her to write something in my journal. She wrote (in Spanish, of course): "To a very nice gentleman, I hope you have a great time on the Camino de Santiago." Pretty cool.

It was a long, long overnight flight, and I was probably the only passenger who did not sleep at all. Not one bit. I tried, but it just wasn't happening. I had a little bag with me, containing all the essentials for a long flight that I'd read about – saline nasal spray, ear plugs, Tylenol PM – and I dutifully used all those things. But my restless leg syndrome and my anxiety kicked in, and so I stood beside my seat for awhile, walked up and down the aisle for awhile, stood at the back of the plane for awhile, sat for awhile, stood for awhile, sat for awhile.

Finally, we landed at Barajas and I went through customs and got my passport stamped, picked up my black duffel bag containing my backpack, hiking shoes and trekking pole, and headed outside the terminal. People on the Camino chat forum had told me exactly what to do to get to Pamplona, but I didn't write anything down. I don't know why I didn't write myself some reminders. I just didn't. Didn't even think about it. I guess I thought I knew what to do. It sounded easy, but as soon as I stepped outside, I promptly forgot everything I'd been told.

I thought I'd be able to take a bus straight from the airport to Pamplona, but I could not find one. Buses were everywhere and were bound for a wide array of cities, but none for Pamplona that I could find. I'm tired as hell, probably jet-lagged, kind of brain-dead, and dragging this increasingly heavy duffel bag around, back and forth, up and down, trying to figure out how to get where I need to be. I asked a few airport people standing around, but they weren't real helpful. Severe communication breakdown. I'm getting a little exasperated at this point, wondering if I'll ever find the right bus. Is there a right bus? What am I doing to do? Finally, I remember something about looking for a bus no. 200, and I spot one, way over there. I walk over and say something to the driver about going to Pamplona. The expression on my face must have given away my growing desperation, and the pretty young girl sitting behind the wheel smiled and said in English, "Take this bus, get off at the last stop and go upstairs."

Big smile. "Gracias." I was so relieved.

The bus took me to the downtown bus station, and I followed a crowd up a long set of stairs and found the ticket sales area. I waited in line for several minutes, stepped up to a window and was not-so-politely told that I needed to take a number. Normally, that probably would have pissed me off pretty good. But now, so tired and disoriented, I obediently turned and walked to the number-dispensing machine, pulled a ticket and got back in line. When it was my turn again, I said, "Pamplona," handed over about 25 euros, got my bus ticket and sat down to wait for the 3 o'clock bus.

As the time crawled by, my mind started to get the best of me again. I watched people walking around, talking on cell phones, and all I could think about was how very far away I was from home. Sitting in sort of a dingy bus station somewhere in downtown Madrid, knowing absolutely nobody. I had decided not to take a phone with me, and rely on calling cards if I needed to make a call, so I was truly all alone. Part of what I wrote in my journal while I sat there included, "I'm really pretty much freaking out." I was basically home-free at this point, but ... would the bus be here on time? Would it be late? Would I get on the right bus? What if I miss the bus?

I kept thinking, "What have you done? What were you thinking? Why in the hell did you come here?" I tried not to think about how far I actually was from home. I walked outside several times to where the buses come in, to check and re-check the bay number for my bus. Stood out there for awhile. Went back inside and sat on a bench. Rustled around in my duffel bag a little bit. Watched the clock. Bought a bottle of water from a vending machine. Listened to the garbled arrival and departure announcements that I could not fully understand. Finally, around 2:30 p.m., I walked outside and just stood there.

Sure enough, the bus was right on time. I watched as other people walked around and slid their bags into the big luggage compartment on the outside of the bus. So I queued up and heaved my duffel bag in there, showed the driver my ticket and climbed aboard. Now, I'm feeling a little better, but still a bit nervous about a transfer I have to make in some place called Soria. The bus is big and new and nice, and it's a pleasant, comfortable trip. Two seats ahead of me is a mother and her teenage son. She's a hottie and he's a good-looking kid, probably about 16 or 17, who has a cell phone plugged into a laptop computer and seems to be skyping or something most of the trip. He turns the open laptop to face the window, holds it close to his face and carries on a whispered conversation with somebody. Pretty interesting.

Eventually, I arrive at the Pamplona bus station, meet my Spanish angel and check in at the hotel. When I turned the key (an actual key; not a magnetic card) and opened the door to my room, I was a little surprised at how small it was – roughly the size of a large walk-in closet, with a tiny bathroom and a small window looking out on a brick wall. Wow. I'd heard European hotel rooms were small, but ….

After exploring the Plaza, walking around in the rain and buying some sandwich-makings and two tall cans of San Miguel, I returned to my miniature room, ate dinner while sitting on the bed and watching some Spanish TV news stations, then took a warm bath in the itty-bitty tub. The thing couldn't have been much more than two feet wide and four feet long. It was really small. But I really like baths, so I filled it up with hot water and wedged my six-feet, two-inches in there. It was comforting. Kind of pitiful, I guess, but comforting. After that, I took out my Camino guidebook and looked at a small map of the central part of the city, and made plans for the next day. I have decided to stay here an extra night, to recuperate from the travel day and rest up for the start of my Camino.

June 10

*A*fter a nice meal of Paella at an outdoor cafe on the Plaza del Castillo, I sat on a park bench watching some little girls play ball. Sunshine is breaking through the clouds, and the wind is light and cool. It is about 7 o´clock and, as always, the Plaza is busy, busy, with walkers, skaters, bicyclers. As I sit and watch, suddenly the green plastic ball comes bouncing my way. I reach out with my left foot and stop it. One of the little girls, very cute with a long ponytail, skips up and grabs the ball. "Gracias," she says, and smiles brightly. Wow. A simple smile and the sunshine makes my day.

Tomorrow, I head out on the Camino. The start of a 420-mile journey to reach Santiago, and to find along the way ... we shall see ...

Standing in front of the Hemingway statue on Pamplona's Plaza del Castillo

Awoke from a decent night's sleep and fixed a cup of coffee in my room while I got ready to go out. Breakfast is included with the room, so I head downstairs and find a nice buffet, with scrambled eggs, two kinds of ham, bacon, orange juice, coffee, chocolate croissants, fresh fruit and more. The tables are covered with white linen cloths, there are nice china plates, cups and saucers, sparkling silverware, soft music is playing and it is all sort of elegant. I sit at a corner table and write in my journal while I eat.

Then it's back up to my room to grab my day-pack and take a look around. First, I head for the bullring and the famous Ernest Hemingway statue. Hemingway is my literary hero. I really like his style of writing. I love the books, "The Old Man and the Sea" and "The Sun Also Rises," which is set in Pamplona. I find the large bullring stadium easy enough, but miss the statue the first time around. I apparently walked right past it, but finally I see it and I walk up and ask a woman standing there if she will take a picture of me standing in front of it. She does, and I thank her.

I also find the famed Estefeta street, site of the annual San Fermin festival's Running of the Bulls, which Hemingway chronicled in "The Sun Also Rises." To actually be standing in the place I'd read about so many times is unbelievably cool. The street is very narrow and enclosed on both sides by shops and stores and apartments. I imagine what it must be like running along this street ahead of a herd of stampeding bulls. A car comes along now and then, and I have to step aside to give it room to pass. I take some pictures and head back across the Plaza and look for signs of the Camino. Just like it says in everything I read before I got here, the pathway is marked by yellow arrows, and the guidebook shows where it tracks through the center of Pamplona, so I find it fairly easily. I spot a disheveled-looking guy with a backpack, looking around while holding a map in his hands, and I say, "Camino?" He says in a thick accent, "You speak French?" I say, no, and we smile and shrug our shoulders and go our separate ways.

I follow Camino waymarkings out of the old city and through the more modern downtown area. There are lots of signs along the way, and I also see a few other people with backpacks heading the same direction. I continue through a park and on a little further, until I decide that I know enough now to at least get started tomorrow. I turn around and head back the way I came. I'm concerned that if I stray too far, I might get lost.

I can't remember if it was the first day I arrived or the second, but I do remember my first attempt to get some cash from an ATM. That had also been part of my research — what to do about cash. Don't worry about it, people said, there are ATMs everywhere, and you just use your bank card from home when you get there. Grab cash as you need it. No problem. I had taken about 80 euros with me, thanks to a local bank currency exchange back home, so I wouldn't have to worry about it right away, but I was a little nervous when I stuck my ATM card in one of the machines just outside the Plaza. Please don't keep my card; please don't keep my card.

I slid the card in, followed the instructions, pushed a few buttons and viola! it worked. Euros came out; my card came back out; and I got a receipt. Phew. OK. I usually got two- or three-hundred euros at a time, and I only had to get cash three or four times while I was there. Fees for the transactions were minimal. A few bucks here and there.

Anyway, it's around noon when I get back to the Plaza, and I take a seat on one of the benches. I watch as people are walking, walking, walking. Old men sitting around talking; some walking dogs. People riding bicycles; pushing babies in strollers. It is a busy place.

I want to strike up a conversation with someone, and see how my rusty Spanish holds up. I figure an old man is probably the safest bet, and there are lots of them around, but I can't work up the nerve to approach anybody. Finally, a kindly-looking gent walks up and sits on the opposite end of my bench. I say, "Hola," or "Como esta?" or something, and he smiles and returns my greeting. We begin to talk and I tell him that I am from Texas, and he asks if I am here for the Camino. I say, yes, and explain that I plan to start the next day and walk as far as Puente la Reina, a town roughly 26 kilometers away. I've easily walked 20 kilometers during my training, so I figure 26 kilometers is plenty doable. He tells me that is too far a distance for my first day's walk, and advises me to not push too hard, and to consider stopping sooner. I've heard the same advice from other people during my research. Don't push too hard in the beginning. I pull out my guidebook and he tells me it would be better to stop at some place like Obanos, before I get to Puente la Reina. I thank him and say I will consider it.

The old man says he has always lived in Pamplona, and never been to the United States. We talk about all the pretty girls in Pamplona – my goodness, they're everywhere – and he smiles and says, yes, they are arriving in anticipation of the famous San Fermin festival next month. It will be a wild place then, he says, with lots of thieves and pickpockets around, lots of excitement and craziness. I'm glad I will be hundreds of miles away by that time. I should be in Santiago by then …

June 11

A *pleasant walk through Pamplona's city streets, through a gorgeous park where crowds of kids are laughing and playing, past the university and into the beautiful countryside. A cool breeze blows and several people wish me, "Buen Camino," as we cross paths in and around the campus. A fine start to a fine day.*

Then, the route turns uphill — seriously uphill, an apparent climb of more than 300 meters in elevation over about a four-kilometer stretch, to the site of a towering wind turbine farm. That's pretty darn steep. I'm about halfway up a brutal climb, along a narrow dirt path strewn with slippery stones, to Alto del Perdon (Hill of Forgiveness) and the peregrino monument, huffing and puffing, wondering if this torture is ever going to end. This backpack must weigh 30 pounds! My left shoulder is aching and my legs are heavy.

As I stop for one of several quick breathers along the way, I look down and spot a cute little lady bug, working furiously to climb her own little mountain. Slipping and sliding along tall blades of grass, turning around and climbing some more. I take it as a sign, and dig my trekking pole into the ground and push on. At the top, finally, after several more rest stops, I pause and take a picture of the monument. It is beautiful here, and you can see the city, far back in the distance. I sit for a few minutes and take off my backpack, before heading off again. Now, the path turns downhill — thank goodness — but it doesn't get any easier. My pack is still heavy and uncomfortable, and the path is completely covered with loose, slippery stones of all shapes and sizes for several more miles. It is slow going.

Nearly 20 kilometers from where I began, I arrive at paradise – a beautiful new albergue in a place called Uterga. I'm hot and tired and ready to stop. When I walk in and ask, "Hay camas?" and the pretty senorita smiles and says, "Si," I am a very happy ol´ man.

Pilgrim's monument atop the Alto de Perdon (Hill of Forgiveness), just outside Pamplona

Last night was not a good night. Not a good night at all. I was awake from probably two in the morning to at least 5 o'clock, tossing and turning, coming very close at times to seriously freaking out. At one point, I was afraid I was going to have some sort of panic attack, or anxiety attack. Completely lose control of my mind and body, and start hyperventilating, or going into some serious heart palpitations or something. The walls were closing in, and all I could think about was how far away from home I was, how completely and utterly alone I felt, and that in the morning I had to get out of this hotel room and walk – by myself – out of the city and into the countryside. To where? Where am I going? What the hell am I doing here?

My anxiety grew and grew to the point that I started taking slow, deep breaths, again and again, and literally talking to myself out loud. "You're OK, John. You're OK, John. You're going to be OK. Let yourself fall asleep. It's OK." Over and over, I tried to calm myself down. Finally, after taking a couple of generic Tylenol PMs, I slept for about three hours, I think, and woke up about 8 o'clock. Washed my face and brushed my teeth and all that good stuff, got my backpack ready to go and headed downstairs for breakfast. Here's part of what I wrote in my journal as I ate at the same corner table:

"Well, today I begin. I'm not terrified like I was last night, but I'm definitely nervous. I can feel it. I'll be glad when it's two or three days from now, and I feel more comfortable. I sure hope I feel more comfortable."

After checking out of the hotel, I strap on my backpack and step outside, turn right and head across the Plaza, the same way I rehearsed it yesterday. Through the city streets, past the beautiful park full of laughing children, across the university campus and into the countryside. So far, so good. A young couple with backpacks on walks ahead of me, but I lose sight of them when I stop on a little stone footbridge over a stream to try and adjust my backpack. I don't know how much the damn thing weighs, but it is really heavy. Too heavy, I know, but I honestly don't think I have a lot of surplus gear. People on the Camino chat forum I joined several months ago recommended taking as little stuff as possible, and keeping the pack lighter than 20 pounds. Mine must weigh at least 25 pounds, and probably more. I left a couple of things back in the hotel room, including a paperback copy of "The Sun Also Rises," to try and make it lighter, but it still seems awfully heavy.

I continue on and make my way through Cizur Menor, a small, very pretty little town a few kilometers outside Pamplona. After that, it's out into the country. Nothing but fields, and mountains in the distance. Large, white wind turbine blades slowly spinning on top of the far-away mountains. That's where I'm headed. As I reach the edge of town and cross the last paved street, I spot a big, yellow arrow painted vertically on a silver streetlight pole, pointing toward a narrow dirt path leading into a grassy field. Just like they said – follow the yellow arrows. OK, deep breath, here we go.

This is where I hear my first "Buen Camino," from people apparently out for a walk and heading back to town. This happens a lot during the coming weeks – locals using parts of the Camino path for a walking trail. I knew about the traditional Buen Camino greeting from my research, but actually hearing it for the first time is somehow moving. It sounds genuine, and kind of reassuring. Strangers from half-a-world away, people you will never see again, crossing your path for an instant, and wishing you well. "Have a good Camino, my friend. Welcome." It is nice, and I return their greetings with "Gracias," and I think maybe this is going to be OK after all.

The path continues to meander through the field, gradually making its way toward the wind turbines. It's pretty and the weather is beautiful, and I'm walking. Just walking. Not too bad. Everything is going OK. I stop in a little village called Zariquiegui and sit on a park bench and watch a couple of kids kick a ball back and forth, while I fix a sandwich with leftovers from the night before. I slice my thumb open a little with the new Swiss army knife I bought for the trip, but it's not too bad. I eat and replenish my water supply from an outdoor fuente, where a group of people on bicycles are also watering up.

The path eventually starts heading a little bit uphill, but the walking is easy and the views back toward Pamplona are incredible. My shoulder is aching and my legs are a little tired, but things are going pretty well. I don't see anybody else at all. Finally, I run into the young couple I saw back at the university. They are resting and taking pictures near a park bench alongside the path. I decide to take a break, too, wondering if this is the Alto del Perdon. I ask the girl if she would mind taking a picture of me with my camera, and she happily obliges. I sit for a few minutes and then press on, up the hill. Up the hill. Up the hill.

Finally, without realizing it, I suddenly reach the top and see the wrought-iron monument to the medieval pilgrims. Wow, I actually made it. Another peregrino is there, a young man, sitting on a concrete slab, resting. That looks like a helluva good idea, and after taking a few pictures, I slide my backpack off and sit on another part of the slab. Goodness gracious, as I wrote later in my journal – that was absolutely brutal. No other way to describe it. I thought that after working up to 20 kilometers during my training walks at home, I was ready. But this hike is nothing like walking alongside the highway back in Texas. I'm tired already, and I've only gone probably 12-13 kilometers.

A little more rest and I gear back up and continue on. This time, the path turns sharply downhill. The terrain is really rugged and covered with all shapes and sizes of smooth, slippery stones. It is impossible to step on a solid, stable surface. You are slipping and sliding all the time. Someone told me later that the descent here was frightening. I hadn't thought about it at the time, but he was right – slip and fall hard, and you could definitely be in trouble. I took it slow and picked my way carefully along, using my trekking pole for balance and made it to level ground.

Before long, I entered a small village and soon spotted an "albergue" sign on my left. It was a beautiful building and, at this point, looks to me like paradise. I'm exhausted. It's about 3:30 in the afternoon and I've had enough for one day. I figure out later that I've only gone about 10.5 miles in about six hours, but I'm done.

I walk through the gate and past the large patio with tables and chairs and umbrellas, through the front door and into a blessedly cool bar/restaurant area. It is nice and clean and wonderful. A pretty senorita is behind the counter, and I ask, "Hay camas?" This is the proper way to ask whether there are any beds available, according to my guidebook. If there are no beds, that means I will have to turn around and keep walking, and hope to find a bed at the next place, wherever that is. But the dark-haired senorita smiles and says, "Si," and I am a very happy man.

I show my pilgrim's credentials, pay a total of 22 euros for a bed for the night and a three-course "pilgrim's menu" dinner special. I have read all about these pilgrim's meals in my research, and they're supposed to be a really good deal. What the heck, I say, and I'm not altogether sure I have a choice, other than to hit the road again and try to find something to eat. And, really, I don't care. I actually survived the first day, made it to shelter, and I just want to eat and go to bed.

The young lady – who speaks a little English, but not much – shows me to the dormitory. She instructs me very politely to leave my dusty shoes under a bench in the foyer, where there are already about 10 pairs of hiking boots and shoes lined up. Then we head upstairs, through a good-size sitting area with couches, chairs and two computers that offer Internet access at 30 minutes for one euro. Then there's a large coed dorm with probably a dozen bunk beds, and separate bathrooms and showers for men and women. I mention that the bathroom facilities are separate, because such is not always the case. As I am soon to find out, in some places the bathrooms and showers are shared by men and women. Not just shared, but used at the same time, by anyone and everyone. Interesting.

So I claim a bottom bunk in the corner of the room by unrolling my lightweight blue sleeping bag across the mattress, unpack my shower stuff and clean clothes, and head for the shower. The bathroom is nice, clean, and the shower feels oh so good. I finish my shower, put on fresh clothes, stuff my dirty ones in a plastic bag, hang my towel off the edge of my bunk and square away my backpack, then head into the sitting room and spend a little time blogging on the Internet and e-mailing home. Back at the hotel in Pamplona, there was a laptop and free Internet service in the lobby, and I started a blog during my two days there. I also logged on to Expedia.com at one point and checked to see how much it would cost me to turn around and go back home. I seriously did.

There was a small library of paperbacks on a shelf above the computer station there at Uterga, and I left a copy of my book, Finding God in Texas, among the two dozen or so others. I had brought several copies with me on the trip, and left a couple in airport bookstores and at a couple of the albergues along the way. Why not? Two or three of my books made it to Spain, and somebody may have even read them. Eventually, I headed downstairs to wait for dinner, which is to be served at 7 p.m.

A few minutes later, the pretty senorita announces dinner time and I head for the dining room, where three other people are also waiting to eat. She asks if we all want to sit together, and is excited when we agree to do so. So we sit at a table for four, and the girl – I can't recall her name – cheerfully describes the pilgrim's dinner menu. We all choose our first course – soup, salad or pasta – and then start introducing ourselves. Across from me is a tall, gray-haired man named Tom, who lives in Spain but speaks with a fairly strong British accent. To my left is a middle-aged woman from Germany and across from her is her husband. I don't remember their names. Everybody speaks English, and there is plenty to talk about, recalling the day's adventure and telling where everybody is from, what we all do back home, things like that. When I say I am from Texas, everybody smiles real big and says, "Oh, Texas!"

This turns out to be the same reaction I get every time I tell someone where I'm from. Everybody from anywhere has heard of Texas. Pretty cool.

We eat and drink wine and talk and laugh and it's a great time. I describe the trouble I had today with my backpack, how heavy the damn thing seemed and how it kept hurting my shoulder. Tom and the German guy both tell me that I need to cinch the waist strap as tight as I possibly can get it. That way, the weight will rest more on my hips than on my shoulders, they explain. They also advise me – after getting their laughter under control – to get rid of the two-pound jar of peanut butter that I'd brought along. Neither one of them can believe I actually packed two pounds of peanut butter, when the whole idea is to make your backpack as light as possible. Some people actually cut unneeded straps and buckles and such off their packs to save ounces of weight. Now, I understand why.

After dinner, we wind up outside on the patio, enjoying the cool evening breeze. I smoke a cigar and chat with Tom for awhile, then everyone starts turning in for the night. Most people want to get an early start in the morning, and these albergues want you out by 8 a.m., anyway. Most of them turn out the lights and lock the doors by 10 p.m.

I head back upstairs and brush my teeth. Birds are chirping outside as I climb into my bunk and try to go to sleep. There are six or eight other people in the room, already in bed, and I'm kind of off to myself, against the back wall. I'm feeling OK, but still finding it really hard to get to sleep. I toss and turn a lot, and when I wake up in the morning, everybody else is already gone. I get dressed and brush my teeth and get my backpack ready, head downstairs and out onto the patio. The morning is cool and still and very quiet.

I buy a paper cup of café con leche from a vending machine on the patio, and pull the big jar of peanut butter out of my backpack, along with a chunk of bread leftover from the day before. Sit down and slather some peanut butter on the bread and have some breakfast. Leave the jar of peanut butter on the table, and away I go. Destination, Puente la Reina …

The end of my first day on the Camino, sitting outside the albergue at Uterga, just west of Pamplona, with fellow pilgrim, Tom Kierulf

June 12

*B*irds are chirping loudly outside the albergue window as the sun comes up. It's the merciful end of another sleepless night, with fear and anxiety once again swirling through my monkey brain. Not as bad as the night before, but enough to keep me awake until the early morning hours. So, I crawl out of my bottom bunk, careful not to thwack my head on that damn metal bar — again! Normal bathroom duties, then square away the backpack and head out for another day on the road.

Scenery is spectacular on the way to Puente la Reina, with the Camino path overlooking dark green mountains and sculptured, golden fields. As I enter the town, I see a few other pilgrims leaving an albergue, taking the day's first steps. A meandering route through the narrow city streets leads past the ancient Church of the Crucifixion (Iglesia del Crucifijo) and over the beautiful medieval stone bridge that crosses the Arga river and out of town, toward Maneru and then a dazzling approach through carefully cultivated vineyards to Cirauqui, a medieval hilltop village that presents a picture-postcard setting as it comes into view.

The road has been fairly easy today, after yesterday's brutal ascent. A fellow peregrino told me, as we paused along a steep and slippery incline, that someone told her 14 people have died along that ascent from Pamplona. Wow, I guess I did all right. Then, as I near the village of

Lorca, the path turns sharply uphill and memories of yesterday return. But I make it unscathed, except for aching legs and sore feet, to a nice albergue, where I decide to rent a private room for the night. The price is 20 euros, which is about three times the cost of a bed in the dorm, but hopefully I'll get some sleep.

Earlier in the day, shortly after leaving Puente la Reina, it occurs to me for some reason the source of my anxiety, the reason for my stress and worry since I've been here. It is due to a feeling of loss of control. I'm way out of my comfort zone, and too far away from it to rush back and feel safe again. I can't just jump in the car and drive home. I'm stuck here. And it occurs to me that this is a lesson for my entire life. I don't like to not have control. A place for everything and everything in its place. Routine. No sudden changes. Smooth sailing in familiar waters. Unfortunately, I also know that control is really an illusion.

Free wine fountain outside a church to fortify pilgrims walking the Camino

Approaching the picturesque medieval village of Cirauqui

OK, today I relaxed a bit a little bit and enjoyed myself. As I wrote in my journal, the scenery was absolutely incredible. Puente la Reina is a beautiful little city, and the approach about seven kilometers later to Cirauqui was breathtaking, it really was. Carefully manicured vineyards alongside the Camino, the dirt path winding its way up to the tiny village perched high atop the hill. My legs are really, really sore, but I just sort of get into a walking rhythm and keep putting one foot in front of the other.

I have no idea where I'm heading today, really, just following the path. I have my guidebook, of course, with its little maps and descriptions and such, but I don't yet have a feel for what I'm doing. As the days go by, I start to figure out that 20 kilometers walking is a pretty good day, and 25 kilometers is a really good day. So I start to be able to sort of plan out the day, and pick a destination. For now, I just walk.

Another six or so kilometers past Cirauqui, I walk into Lorca, a beautiful little town, with narrow cobblestone streets going up and down, this way and that, old stone buildings all over the place. After yesterday's climb, today was fairly easy until I started getting close to Lorca. Then things turned uphill again. These uphill stretches are a bear. By the time I get there, I've had enough for the day, with 20.2 kilometers covered since I left Uterga. I come to an albergue that offers private rooms, and I decide to get one. It's 20 euros for the night, and I'm thinking maybe I'll get some sleep in a room by myself. I haven't slept much since I got here four days ago.

The so-called private room turns out to be sort of semi-private, but it is still pretty nice. The room is upstairs, above the bar, adjacent to the small dormitory (eight beds, maybe?), and I have to share a bathroom with everybody else. But it is twice the size of my hotel room back in Pamplona, has two large comfortable beds, and the place is nice and quiet, except for a raucous kid's birthday party out on the street below that lasts most of the afternoon. But that's OK. I take a nice shower, put on fresh clothes, wash my dirty clothes in the bathroom sink and hang them out the window of my room, go downstairs and drink a cold beer, then spend some time on their computer, checking email and blogging a little bit. Talked to some young guy from Michigan or somewhere up north who is staying in the dorm, and he smiles real big like everybody else does when I tell him I'm from Texas. He says something about my southern accent.

I go down and sit on a bench outside the albergue to smoke a cigar and drink another beer. This ice-cold San

Miguel draft beer is really good. Otra cerveza grande, por favor. How much was a large beer? Two euros? Two-fifty? Something like that. Anyway, that's when I met Jytte, a very nice woman from Denmark, who was staying at an albergue across the street. I was sitting, watching people come and go, when she walked up and sat down. She speaks English and we talk for awhile about this and that. It is her second time on the Camino, she explained. I didn't know it at the time, of course, but Jytte was to become an important part of my Camino experience, and we remain friends to this day.

I don't remember now what I did for dinner that night — probably had the pilgrim's menu in the bar — but I turned in early, feeling a lot better than when I started.

June 13

S itting in a bar on top of a mountain, just finished a dinner with new friends from South Africa, Holland, England and Norway! Today was a short, fairly easy walking day that ended with a 2-kilometer climb up the mountain. It was worth it, though, for the stunning panoramic views. I got my first taste early this morning of tortilla y patatas (I think that's right), which is sort of an omelet quiche-type thing made of eggs and potato that is very good. And tonight will be an experience for the ages. Sleeping in a small dorm room with about eight other men, in bunk beds. One little dude who is in the top bunk above me was snoring his ass off as he napped this afternoon, even as people shuffled in and out of the room, wrangling backpacks, talking, changing clothes. I have some good earplugs and I'm pretty tired, but for some strange reason, I don't think I'll be enjoying a very restful night. From the looks of things, it promises to be a symphony of sound, as I try and get comfortable on a cheap three-by-six plastic mattress. Oh, well, it is what it is, all part of the deal. Buen Camino!

This is one of the places I mentioned earlier that features coed bathroom facilities. Villamayor de Monjardin. It sits 650 meters atop a mountain and is a wonderful, beautiful place, featuring a 12th century church and castle ruins. I find an albergue across the plaza from the church, and a small group of people is sitting outside around a patio table. I approach them and a guy with long blonde hair looks at me, smiles and says, "Warm day, isn't it?" Indeed.

These people manage the albergue, and they explain that registration to spend the night opens at 4 o'clock, and it is shortly after noon right now, but they let me take my stuff upstairs and take a shower. I'm not sure what this building originally was, but the rooms are teeny-tiny and the ceilings are low. I have to duck my head to climb the stairs from the front room, and be careful as well not to bump my head when I step across the threshold into the bunkroom.

There are three or four rooms at the top of the narrow staircase, surrounding a small bathroom, with several toilets on one side, a sink and mirror, and three showers on the other side. Men and women use all these facilities at the same time, it turns out. For the Europeans, I think, this is nothing much out of the ordinary. They come and go throughout the afternoon and early evening, taking care of their business. One very large fellow from France is limping around in nothing but a pair of sandals over heavily bandaged feet and some very tight briefs that are nowhere near large enough to cover what needs to be covered. Modesty is impossible, and apparently no one cares, anyway. But it's a first for me, for sure, sitting on a toilet while a woman from Germany or wherever is taking a shower and another female is at the sink three feet away, brushing her teeth.

I only walked 14.6 kilometers today, but it was pretty rugged, including the climb up here. My body is tired, and my legs are aching, but I write in my journal that I think I'll be turning a corner soon, as far as fitness goes, and things will soon start getting easier.

After I shower and change – I put my dirty clothes in a plastic bag to save for washing tomorrow – I wander over to the bar next door for a cold beer and a delicious tortilla y patata. I sit at a picnic table outside under an umbrella, and I'm feeling pretty darn good. I'm hoping my legs will recover somewhat by tomorrow, so I can put in a longer day on the road. But I'm satisfied with my progress and, really, I'm doing pretty good, distance-wise. According to the guidebook, I'm almost right on schedule for three days of walking.

Other people start drifting over to the bar, and a young Spanish guy with a plate of food in his hands sits across from me and introduces himself. Edorta is a really nice guy from San Sebastian, down south, who is here working in the fields, operating some sort of farm machinery. He speaks absolutely no English, and my Spanish is not the greatest, but we manage a pretty decent conversation. He is married to a hairstylist and has two kids. When I tell him that I am a school teacher, he is impressed and talks about how difficult a job that must be. We talk about lack of discipline and lack of respect for adults and such, and he says kids are little smartasses everywhere now, including Spain, and he thinks it is due to the Internet and them getting too much information at too young an age. A lot of truth in that.

My new friend, Tom, eventually makes his way up here and we sit for awhile outside the bar, talking and drinking beer. Then, a pretty young English girl he met somewhere along the way walks up and joins us. Her name is Paula, and she is in sort of a state, a little frazzled, and she proceeds to tell us about being followed through the woods earlier by a strange-looking man on her way here. He was keeping a short distance behind her and hiding behind trees, she said, until she spotted a paved road and ran to it. She didn't see the man after that, but the experience left her pretty shook up.

Paula has a delightful British accent, and is a lively story-teller. She rolls her own cigarettes with flavored tobacco and wears a flowery straw hat over dark pigtails. Personally, I think she is a little full of shit and maybe likes to entertain people with a wee bit of a tall tale, but she is very nice and charming. We wind up spending a lot of time together over the next couple of weeks – Tom, Paula and I – and after we get to know each other a little better, I figure out that she is not full of shit after all, but just a true free spirit. She is truly a modern-day flower child who fearlessly travels the world by herself. She's a trained dancer and a musician who has been all over the place with just a backpack, traveling across India and living for a time in a tree house on the beach in Thailand. She has worked as a magician's assistant, and as a dancer on a cruise ship. Her goal in life is to live off the land somewhere, in a teepee.

Later on, we all have dinner at the albergue, which is staffed by volunteers from a Dutch ministry who cook and serve and clean up. There are about 30 people from all over the world sitting together at long tables, and I mostly chat with a tall, pretty, blonde albergue volunteer from Holland and another attractive woman from South Africa. The girl from Holland tries to talk with me about Jesus and the Bible, as this is basically a ministry for them. She is nice, and I don't mind it. After dinner, I give her a signed copy of my book.

Meanwhile, Verity, the girl from South Africa, is pretty entertaining, with her somewhat refined aristocratic-type manner and accent. She talks of living in Zimbabwe with her parents and servants and such, and says this is her second time to walk the Camino. She tells a really cool story about the Camino experience, beginning to end, being like a spiritual rebirth, which indeed it proved, and is continuing to prove, to be.

After dinner, I walked back over to the bar to use their computer – the standard one euro for 30 minutes of Internet service – to do some blogging and emailing and such. While I was at the bar, I missed the after-dinner meditation time, which I really was looking forward to, but afterward, I sat out on the Plaza with Tom and smoked a cigar, feeling relaxed and pretty good about everything. After three days, I've gotten a little better feel for the walking and am able to estimate and plan the rest of my journey a little bit, which is comforting. I probably feel a little more in control again, not quite as helpless. I've gotten more used to using the guidebook and so I can figure out basically when I'll be where, so maybe that removes some of the anxiety.

In my journal, I have an entry marked 8:50 p.m. that says:

"Fear appears to be gone, and I feel very comfortable. Relaxed and happy. Many good conversations with people from Spain, England, Norway, South Africa. I even "talked" with a guy from France just now about the massive blisters all over his feet. I didn't understand a word he said, but apparently he is in a lot of pain and suffering circulation problems in his legs. I think he is looking for a way to get back home. Later on, I find out that he was unable to continue, and did indeed find a way to go back home.

Today, I was walking alone, on a wide, flat dirt and gravel pathway, and I began to feel a part of the Camino. It's hard to explain. It was just a feeling inside. Like I was a part of the Camino. Maybe it's really God, working through the Camino. That would mean, maybe, that I was feeling closer to God? I don't know. Maybe it's the spirit of the millions of people before me who have walked this same pathway. To think I'm actually stepping in the footsteps of people who walked this way for hundreds and hundreds of years is amazing. I've been asking God to be with me as I walk, so who knows …

A girl from South Africa was talking (earlier) about how the Camino changes you, about its spirituality. She said a lot of things that

I've read before, and that I've heard other people say. I am feeling things already, so I'm looking forward to everything this journey brings. No. 1, I got past that crazy fear that nearly overwhelmed me in the beginning. No. 2, I finally understand a little bit about the illusion of control, and the feeling of losing that imaginary control. I'm meeting and talking with really nice and interesting people from any number of other countries, and they don't think I'm weird, or an idiot. They actually seem to like me, in fact.

The breeze is cool. The sky is blue over the mountains. Birds are chirping and circling as another day comes to an end. I feel good. Relaxed. De-stressing. I'm how many thousand miles from home, and I'm OK."

June 14

*B*irds — *swallows?* — *are circling, circling, circling the medieval church tower in Torres del Rio, a half-day walk from Villamayor de Monjardin. I've decided to stop here for today, mostly due to a nasty blister on the bottom of my left foot. The legs are feeling much better now, but this damn blister hurts! If nothing else pops up once this thing heals, it should be a lot smoother sailing.*

Something interesting I noticed during my walk today. A lot of people in Spain have these huge dogs. I'm not sure of the breed, but they're big. They've all been either behind a fence or tethered, and when they bark, it sounds like ...

"WOOF-O!" You get it? Not woof. Woof-o. OK, never mind. Meanwhile ...

Today's spiritual moment occurred shortly after daybreak, as I sat outside the albergue in Monjardin, waiting for Tom to come out and join me at the bar next door for a little cafe con leche and some desayuno. I watch as a few early birds come out of the albergue and gear up, adjusting their backpacks and lacing up boots, and head off into the morning mist for the day's walk. What is in their mind today? What are they thinking about? What are they seeking? What do they hope to find along the Camino? The feeling I have is hard to identify ... humility, perhaps? Feeling like a part of the human race; a sense of belonging? All these different people from different parts of the world, brought together at the same time in this place, many for the same reason(s).

Last night, I sat at dinner across from a woman from South Africa. Her name is Verity (which means truth). This is her second Camino, and she explained that the journey includes four stages: first, from the Pyrenees mountains and through Pamplona (where I started) is like one's birth and early childhood, a difficult time in which you struggle, learn to walk, etc.; then, you begin to find your stride and a rhythm as confidence grows and strength increases; then, on the long, hot, dry meseta, the old self begins to slowly die away; followed by a rebirth as you enter the province of Galicia and approach Santiago de Compostela, burial place of St. James, where a new person emerges.

This is only my fourth day on the Camino, but I can say that I feel at peace here. It has been difficult so far, but I'm beginning to find my rhythm and stride, and starting to let go and let the Camino guide me. It is an amazing place.

Me, Tom and Paula rest outside a bar in Viana

Oh, this blister. I didn't know it at the time, of course, but it was to become one of the defining parts of my entire Camino experience. I had read a lot about blisters and the importance of taking care of the feet, but like pretty much everything else, when I got here, I forget all the good advice people gave me. It started out as a small "hotspot," right in the middle of the ball of my left foot. It was a little uncomfortable, and I was concerned about it, but I wasn't quite sure what it was, because it didn't really look like a blister. Is this one of those hotspots I read about during my research, or is my foot just kind of irritated, or what? It's a little red and tender, about a half-inch long and eighth-inch wide.

When I met Tom back in Uterga, one of the things he talked about at dinner was being mad at himself for letting not just one, but both of his feet get badly blistered. He started his journey back in Roncesvalles, which is about 40 kilometers from Pamplona, near the border with France, and said he was in a lot of pain. I didn't think I really had anything to worry about, because I was wearing special moisture-wicking hiking socks that are supposed to help prevent blisters, and I hadn't had any trouble during my training hikes, so I thought I was good to go.

Just in case, I stop at a farmacia in some little village – I don't remember which one – and ask the pharmacist to take a look at my foot. She agrees, but tells me (in Spanish) that she will only look at it, and that she cannot treat it. That's fine. I sit down, take off my shoe and sock, and she looks and agrees that a Compeed bandage will take care of the problem. So I buy a package of Compeed, for some ridiculous price of 13 euros or something, and I stick one on there. I've read about these bandages, and they are supposed to work like magic for these so-called hotspots.

The thing is triangular-shaped, about the size of a 50-cent piece, and sort of the consistency of silicone or something. Kind of soft and plasticky. You stick it on the hotspot and forget about it – supposedly – and it protects the irritation and eventually takes care of it.

Well, I found out later – much later – that Compeed apparently works great for some people, and not so great for others. I was definitely one of the others. Not only did it not take care of the hotspot, but the thing soon ballooned into a deep, giant blister the same exact shape and size of the damn bandage. It was huge! And it hurt like hell. I cannot begin to describe the discomfort. Walking became excruciating. Each step was incredibly painful, and my entire foot ached and throbbed all the time.

The albergue at Torres del Rio, meanwhile, was fantastic. I got a bed in a four-bunk dorm with Verity and Paula. This was upstairs, and downstairs was a nice patio, washing sink and clothes line for laundry, and separate shower and bathroom facilities for males and females. I limped up and down the stairs, took a shower, put on fresh shorts and T-shirt, washed a bunch of clothes and socks in the big sink on the patio, hung them on the line, bought a cold San Miguel from the hospitalera downstairs, and sat at a picnic table on the balcony, enjoying the view of the 12th century church, Iglesia de Santo Sepulcro, with the sun setting over the mountains behind, and writing in my journal.

I guess this is as good a place as any to talk about clothes washing on the Camino. At the albergues, there is always some sort of washing station outside somewhere. A large sink or two, and maybe a little table on the side, usually a little scrub brush. You just throw your clothes in there, run some water and add whatever kind of soap you have or can borrow. Occasionally, someone leaves soap behind and you can use that. I used a variety of things: hand soap, liquid soap, shampoo. Whatever gets the water a little sudsy.

At first, I tried using the little scrub brushes – scrub, scrub, scrub, rinse, wring, rinse, wring, rinse some more, wring some more – but that was a big pain in the ass, and didn't really seem to be accomplishing much. At some point, I asked Tom about washing clothes, because I didn't know what the hell I was doing, and he said all you can do is just sort of swirl 'em around, agitate 'em a little bit with your hands, and do the best you can to rinse out the day's grime and sweat. Wring 'em out and hang 'em up to dry. OK, cool, that's basically what I had started doing.

Usually one of the last chores of the evening before going to bed is going over to the clothesline to see if things are dry. They usually were, and you grab your stuff and stow it in your backpack. I always slept in my boxer shorts, and had my T-shirt and shorts for the next day ready, along with my shoes and socks.

When I went to bed each night, my backpack was basically ready to go. I'd get up in the morning, take my ear plugs out and put them back in their little plastic case, get my toothbrush and toothpaste out and take care of bathroom duties, then come back to my bunk, have a sit and square everything away, finish getting dressed and off we'd go.

Meanwhile, after a little journal writing and a cold can of beer, I walk – limp – back down the hill and find Tom sitting outside another albergue, and we make plans for dinner, at a restaurant farther down the hill. For the life of me, I can't remember details about dinner that night, either. Most likely, we had the pilgrim's menu, which usually ran about 10 euros and always consisted of three courses. Generally, it would be something like soup or salad, then some kind of entrée like beef or chicken or spaghetti or something, and then a variety of dessert choices. One thing the meals almost always included was fried potatoes. A cheap staple on the pilgrim's menu.

The next morning, I made my way back down the hill for breakfast, and Tom showed up about the time I finished eating. We were planning to walk together today, but he told me to go ahead and get started, and we'd meet up later. So I took off and he eventually caught up to me, when I stopped at a bar in a beautiful little place called Viana.

Paula and I arrived there about the same time and dropped our backpacks outside the same little bar, so I asked if I could join her, and she said, sure. We sat and rested and talked, had a snack from the bar and something to drink. Asked a woman at the next table to take our picture, please. Then, along comes Tom, and he joins us, as well. Another picture, if you don't mind. After about a half-hour or so, we gear up and start the walk to the next town, Logrono.

June 15

*L*ife is simple and good when the sight of a banana and an orange brings a genuine smile to your face.

After a somewhat disappointing "pilgrims breakfast" (cafe con leche, orange juice and toast for 3 euros) at the bar in Torres del Rio, I was heading out for the day's walk when something starting jangling in my pocket. An annoyance that I knew would bother me all day, so I set down my backpack, fished the offender out of my pocket and looked for a better place to stash it.

The first zipper I pulled on the top of my backpack revealed my prize – the fruit I bought the day before and completely forgot about. Now, I was ready to set out for Logrono, the first major milestone along the way to Santiago de Compostela.

Logrono is the first large city we've come to. Described as a "lively university town" of 130,000 people, this marks a little over 92 kilometers I've logged in five days. That's around 55 miles, far below what I anticipated averaging during my planning. Remember, though, that reality slapped me hard in the legs and feet beginning on Day One. Today was my longest day at 20.7 kilometers. I walked nearly the entire way with Tom and Paula, and we were absolutely fried by the time we got to the downtown albergue, basically a temporary warehouse for pilgrims.

But I am feeling good and starting to really enjoy myself, despite the nasty blister on the foot. After a long hike through wine country, I caught up with Paula outside a bar in Viana, population 3,500 and a major pilgrim stop in the 15th century. She had coffee, while I had orange juice and a boccadillo, as we rested our feet at an umbrella-shaded table near the town square. Lots of people were out and about, and we chatted and relaxed, and a few minutes after we sat down, here comes Tom to join us.

As we sat there talking, I marveled at the fact that here I was, a guy from Texas who really hasn't been anywhere to speak of, sitting at an outdoor cafe in Spain, on a gorgeous blue-sky day, with a free-spirited world traveler from England, and a Norwegian-born man who now lives in Spain and speaks English with a refined British accent. Amazing ...

Fresh octopus at a festival in Logrono, a tasty Spanish treat

While it started out as an excellent day, the hike from Viana to Logrono was long and hot and tiring. It's only about a 9.5-kilometer walk, but Logrono is pretty big, and it seemed like it took forever to find our destination after we reached the outskirts of town. Paula had us all singing songs as we walked, which was a lot of fun and helped ease the pain somewhat. Finally, we reached the municipal albergue, a large building in the middle of downtown that contains something like 90 bunk beds on three floors. It was a busy place. We check in, get registered – registration included turning over our passports and retrieving them later, which was a little scary – get our bed assignments, take showers and put on fresh clothes; then Tom and I go outside on the front patio area and soak our feet in this amazing little fountain. It was maybe four feet in circumference, and the water was ankle-deep, cold and felt amazing. We sat there in the afternoon sunshine for at least a half-hour. It was divine. Throughout the day, people sat there and soaked their bare feet.

I took a walk later, a couple blocks over to the plaza area, which is full of bars and restaurants, souvenir shops and clothing stores. I ask a policia if he knows where I can find some cigars and he points me in the right direction, but pretty much everything is closed right now for siesta. Everything just basically shuts down for a few hours in the afternoon. I was walking through some small village one day – can't remember which one – and I stopped at this little hole-in-the-wall tavern for a beer. As he drew my San Miguel, the bartender kept saying something to me that I couldn't quite understand, until finally I figured out that he was telling me that he was leaving to go home for lunch, but I was welcome to sit at one of the outside tables and drink my beer, free of charge. Very cool. So I thanked him, sat down and took my shoes off, as everyone else left, while he locked the place up, got in his car and drove away.

Meanwhile, that evening in Logrono, we had dinner around 7 o'clock at a restaurant a few blocks from the albergue. It was Tom, myself, Paula, Verity, a young German guy whose name I can't recall, and two South African women, Nix and Judy. We sat outside and drank wine, and ate various chicken and beef dishes. The plaza was busy, with people walking here and there, and there was some sort of festival going on across from us. We saw one food booth where they were cooking boiled octopus. A couple of us walked over and took pictures of the guy posing with a steaming octopus on a stick – he'd put it down into the water for awhile, then pull it back out, stick it back in, pull it out – and then Tom walked over and bought a plate of the stuff for everyone to sample. It was cut up in chunks, tentacles and all, covered with olive oil and sweet paprika, served on a bed of potato slices.

I tried a piece, and it was delicious. Not gooey or slimy or rubbery, like you might think, but firm and tender and good. A few weeks later, we had octopus two more times for dinner, when we reached Galicia, where it is considered a specialty item.

After dinner, we sat for awhile at a little park near the albergue, then headed on inside for bed as the sun started going down. I think the curfew was 10 p.m., then they lock the doors and you'd better be inside or you're sleeping outside. Like I said, this place was packed, like a giant can of sardines. Bunks were arranged in little cubicles of four beds each, crammed together in this old stone building, with no air conditioning, no ventilation, no air moving at all. There were a couple of open windows, but it had to have been at least 80 degrees in there all night long.

When the morning came, it was bedlam at 5 a.m. Flashlight beams careening everywhere, dozens of people scurrying back and forth to the bathroom, in and out of the dormitory, up and down the stairs, slinging backpacks around, rushing to get out the door and head to the next stop. Not a very restful place.

Tom and I got up early, as well, and headed out into the city before sunrise. Paula stayed in bed. It was nice, walking in the cool, early morning darkness through the quiet city streets, which reminded me at times of parts of New York City, full of shop after shop locked up tight for the night. I moved on ahead when Tom stopped at an ATM for some cash, and he caught up to me later when I paused to take off my backpack and sit down on a park bench to check the bandage on my left foot. My foot is killing me. Every step is painful, and when I stop, it aches and the whole thing throbs. Better to just keep moving, really.

We have a little trouble finding our way at one point, but a mother-daughter combo from Pennsylvania walking just ahead of us – I met the mom sitting outside the albergue yesterday – found the scallop shell waymarkings in the sidewalk, directing us across a small park and on out of town.

June 16

I t was a day for learning. After a restless night in the downtown Logrono municipal albergue, we set out before dawn, with aching feet and low spirits. As we slog our way through the quiet city streets and head into the countryside, I tell Tom that we surely we are in store for some important lesson. There could be no other reason for this suffering. So we trudge and wince and step slowly along the Camino path, up and down, up and down, for several hours, when Tom stops and turns to me, and says that it occurs to him that there indeed is a lesson to be learned today: that life is easier when it is shared with others. Like yesterday, when he and Paula sang songs for several miles, and quizzed me about country music as I challenged them with song titles. They knew and sang everything! Willie Nelson. Kris Kristofferson. James Taylor. On and on. Our 22-kilometer trek was just as painful as today's was starting out to be, he said, but it did not seem nearly as difficult or unpleasant.

A time later, he mentioned that one of his feet seemed to be improving – both have been painfully blistered for a week – and it occurred to me after he said that, that I have been fortunate to have only one painful foot, instead of two, and I mentioned this to Tom. Of course, I was focusing only on the blistered one, and forgetting to be grateful that my legs feel strong, my back is good, shoulders are fine, and the right foot is great. An excellent example of the way I tend to look at a lot of *things in life, focusing on the negative, forgetting to be grateful for the good things.*

Later, we sit for a rest on a small pile of rocks, in the shade of some small trees and brush, trying to figure out why our minds and bodies are so sluggish today. As we consider the effect of the crowded, hot, cramped sleeping conditions last night, who comes trudging along the path but our little Paula. As it turns out, she is feeling exactly the same way, and we all agree it has to be the negative energy we absorbed from the 90-bed facility, and the mostly ill-tempered crowd with which we shared the place. Gaining at least some insight into the problem seemed to lift our spirits a bit, and we carried on together through Naverrete, and on to our destination for the day at Ventosa, where we discovered a paradise albergue. Small, uncrowded dorm rooms; large showers, bathrooms and laundry room; fully-equipped kitchen; and a beautiful backyard terrace and garden with waterfall, where we enjoyed a delicious pasta dinner prepared by Paula, with slicing and dicing assistance from Tom. All in all, a fine day ... and a fine day for learning.

A home-cooked pasta dinner in Ventosa with new friends (l-r) Tom, Nix, me, Paula, Judy

We had to wait for several hours for the Ventosa albergue to open up, so we found the only place in town that was open, a little bar with plastic tables and chairs outside. Food, drinks, and coin-operated Internet inside. Other people came and went, resting for a bit and then heading for the next stop, but we'd had enough for one day and were content to stay here for the night. I took off my shoes and socks, put on my trusty flip-flops, drank a couple of beers and ate some more delicious tortilla y patatas. Wrote some in my journal and did some e-mailing and blogging on the computer inside.

After awhile, it was time to go check in at the albergue, so we grabbed our gear and headed over there. The place was amazing. When we stepped inside through the beaded curtains, incense was burning and the lights were low, as we lined up to register for the night. The smiling hospitalera took our passports and our seven (maybe eight?) euros, wrote our names down and showed us upstairs to the bedrooms. I saw adjoining rooms full of bunk beds, and ours was on the left, with eight bunks, as I recall, occupied by Tom, me, and two women we did not know. The room had a large window that looked out onto the backyard garden, and the bathrooms – separate facilities for men and women – were huge and clean and nice. The place was equipped with some sort of motion sensors that operated the light switches in the hallways and bathrooms, which came in really handy in the middle of the night.

After taking showers and washing clothes, people began congregating in the backyard, including Nix and Judy, who had saved the day earlier when I turned the corner in some little village and saw them sitting together outside a bar. I was in a lot of pain as I limped up to their table and they said, "Are you all right? You don't look so good." I told them about my foot and asked if they had any pain medication. They said, as a matter of fact, we do, and gave me a sleeve of about a dozen little red and blue capsules, explaining that it was some sort of wonderful over-the-counter painkiller that they had never found anywhere else but South Africa. Judy told me to take two, but to make sure and eat something first. I followed instructions – had some orange juice and a fantastic plate of tortilla y patatas – took two pills and finished the rest of the day relatively pain-free. I could still feel the blister, but it was more uncomfortable than painful, like something thick stuck to the bottom of my foot, and my foot didn't throb and ache nearly as much.

Back at Ventosa, meanwhile, Paula, Tom and I decided to buy some groceries from the albergue's little shop and have ourselves a home-cooked dinner on the patio. We got some pasta, a few fresh tomatoes, a couple bottles of wine, some cheese, garlic, onion, green pepper, olive oil, and other assorted goodies to chop and sauté and mix together. Paula assumed the primary cooking duties, while Tom was responsible for slicing and dicing, and I sort of hung around and stayed out of the way. Judy and Nix – who soon was to become another important part of my Camino and a friend for life – later took care of the clean-up, so basically all I had to do was enjoy the food and the newfound friendship.

We sat for a long time, enjoying the beautiful backyard, and met some more pilgrims, including a young girl from the United States, a big, bearded guy from Germany (what was his name?), and two women also from Germany. I got the usual big-smiles reaction when I told people that I was from Texas, and we all shared things about ourselves and our lives back home, some of the reasons we came to the Camino, stuff like that.

It was a great evening, with wine flowing and lots of laughter and stories, and eventually as night began to fall we all started heading inside to get to bed. As I walked across the patio toward the back door, a deep, heavily-accented voice boomed out behind me, "Goode night, Texas Ranger!" I had to smile. Awesome ...

June 17

*T*oday, *we headed out early from the nicest albergue we've been to so far. The San Saturnino in Ventosa is wonderful. Beautiful building with incense burning as you register; comfortable beds in small, cool rooms; clean, roomy bathroom and showers; washing machine and dryer (for a fee) and hand-washing laundry facilities; fully-equipped kitchen and well-stocked, reasonably-priced tienda with groceries on-premises; incredible backyard patio. Gregorian chanting in the morning to help get you moving.*

Aches and pain — and blisters — are feeling better, and we log a quick 9.4 kilometers to Najera, a beautiful little town of 7,000 that includes a walk across the bridge over the Najerila river and an easy stroll through town. I also bought some stamps for the postcards I wrote four or five days ago!

We press on uphill through poppy fields, vineyards and sunflower fields toward our destination at Ciruena. Both the town and the albergue we find there are a disappointment, but we're not about to keep going after walking 29 kilometers over about nine hours. That included stops for lunch at a bar in tiny Azorfa, and a 15-minute break as Tom and Paula plopped down and soaked their feet in the cool waters of an irrigation channel in some farmer's field. Since I had applied fresh Compeed and assorted other bandages earlier in the day,

I opted for just removing my shoes and socks, giving myself a little foot massage, and putting on clean, dry socks. Aaahhh ...

Since some have asked (people are actually reading this stuff!), I will say that the best places we have stayed so far have been in Uterga, Villamayor de Monjardin and, of course, Ventosa. Lorca is a pretty nice little town and a good stopover, along with Torres del Río. After about a week, and our experience at Logrono, we've decided that avoiding the crowds at the more traditional stops, in favor of the smaller, in-between places provides a much more comfortable, relaxing stay, and better night's rest. Ciao.

Following the Camino out into the countryside

As is always the case, Paula, Tom and I become separated as we head for Najera, a place that provides another picture-postcard photo opportunity as I walk across the bridge into town. As soon as I cross the bridge, I get lost. I'm not sure what happened, but for some reason I decided to take a left and follow the sidewalk, past a row of restaurants and some apartment buildings. I didn't see any signs or waymarkings, but this seemed to be the right way to go. I kept looking for signs and arrows, but after about a kilometer or so, I had the sinking feeling that this was not good.

Up ahead, I spot a man tending a small garden near the street, and I ask him, "Camino este?" I've figured out by now that this basically means, "I'm walking the Camino – is this the right way?" He points me in the opposite direction, and so I head back toward the bridge. A man standing on a second-floor apartment balcony shouts something down at me, and points over toward a half-full parking lot. I wave and cut across that way, and lo and behold, on the side of a building I see a large, yellow painted arrow. A welcome sight indeed.

This town is kinda cool, with narrow, winding streets and lots of people walking around, lots of cars buzzing around. I see a tobacco shop and stop in to buy some stamps for my postcards. Not sure if you can also buy stamps at the post office, but in Spain the place to get stamps is apparently the tobacco shops.

Somewhere along the way, before reaching Azorfa, the three of us come together again. Generally, when you're walking with someone, you may start the day together, and then drift apart, as you get into your own walking rhythm and pace. I had a quicker pace than Tom, and when he sensed me holding back a bit to stay with him, he would often tell me to go on ahead and he would catch up. Sometimes, we would walk and talk together for awhile, sometimes walk together without saying anything, and sometimes one would leave the other behind, giving each a chance to be alone with our individual thoughts.

One day, Tom was really struggling with his painful feet. We had already stopped by a sports shoe store in some little town for him to buy some walking sandals. He was getting discouraged from being in agony all day long, and desperate to find a solution. The sandals helped with the blisters on the top and sides of his feet and toes, but they weren't providing enough protection for the bottoms of his feet. He said he had to be very careful walking to try and avoid stepping on any kind of rock or stone, which was pretty much impossible, especially out in the country.

So one morning, after stopping for breakfast in a town called Fromista, I think it was, Tom took off to another shoe store to look for help. Jytte and I walked on ahead, and wondered if that was the last we were going to see of Tom. He had said that if things didn't improve for him soon, he might have to take a train back to his home in Coruna, on the Atlantic coast of Spain. It was getting pretty serious.

Jytte and I stopped awhile later that day in a little place called Poblacion de Campos. We sat outside a little bar to take a break and rest our feet, and it wasn't long before we see Tom coming toward us, with a bounce in his step and a big smile on his face. We were so excited to see him, and to see him smiling. We clapped our hands, cheering and laughing. Apparently, the guy at the shoe store Tom went to back in Fromista had helped him and he was feeling a lot better. He was back in his hiking boots and rarin' to go.

Meanwhile, a few hours after leaving Azorfa, Tom and Paula and I decided we'd stop for the day in a village called Ciruena. This was one of our longer days, at something like 24.5 kilometers, and the last couple of kilometers were brutal. We walked what seemed like forever through a large, mostly deserted housing development adjacent to a large golf club. It was a hot day, and the all-concrete neighborhood of apartments and townhouses seemed to go on forever. We all thought at one point that we had to be lost. But there was nobody to ask for directions!

We finally found the albergue, though, on the other side of town. It was an old, blue, stone, two-story house, and we knocked on the door and waited. And waited. Finally, someone inside yanked open the metal door with a loud scrape and a clang, and invited us in. The first thing the guy showed us was how to properly open and close the door. You basically had to kind of muscle it. The place was definitely old, but it seemed OK and we were spent. No way we were walking any more today.

The fee here for spending the night is several euros higher than we've been used to, but the isolated location is apparently good for snagging tired pilgrims. Take it or leave it. Supply and demand. It's about six kilometers to the next town, Santo Domingo de Calzada, and the next albergue, and the next town is also one of those large places at the end of the traditional Camino stages outlined in the handbooks. We've already decided to avoid the larger and more hectic facilities in favor of the smaller places, so we're definitely staying put.

We sit at a table in the front room with the owner, Pedro, hand him our passports and pilgrim credentials, and fork over the rather exorbitant fee, and one of the first things out of his mouth is a pretty seriously off-color and racist joke about a black female. We were all a little surprised, since we didn't know this guy and he certainly didn't know us. A little off-color humor among friends is not altogether uncommon, but gee whiz, dude. Along with the fee for a bed and a bath, he also offered us a lentil soup dinner combo for another seven euros or whatever, but Tom quickly declined and we headed upstairs to find a bed and clean up.

There was a small, clean bathroom downstairs and we took turns showering and washing the clothes we had worn that day. Across the dirt road outside, there is a small church with clotheslines in the yard and that's where we hung everything to dry.

After that, we high-tailed it down to the bar, a couple hundred meters away. Some really scruffy-looking dude was asleep in one of the bottom bunks in the room we were assigned, and I hoped that our backpacks would be unmolested when we got back.

June 18

*I*t is getting close to 4 p.m. and I'm sitting in the backyard of a riverside albergue in Villamayor del Rio. Plastic tables and chairs are on the lawn, surrounded by scarlet rose bushes and a large cherry tree, heavy with clumps of ripening fruit. It is quiet here, with a few birds singing in the distance and the wind rustling through a tall stand of poplar trees. For those interested, Tom says he could stay here for a week.

I was tired when I got here an hour ago, feet aching from our 24-kilometer hike today. A lot of climbing, climbing, as always. Then, something happened that was very cool.

As we stepped out the back door and into the yard to relax for awhile, we spotted Nix – the boisterous South African girl we enjoyed a dinner with two nights ago in Ventosa – hanging freshly washed clothes on the line. We were happily surprised because we assumed Nix and her walking companion, Judy, were now outpacing us and we probably would not see them again. After hugs and pleasantries, I asked Nix if she had a needle, since I'd discovered small but wicked-looking blisters on two of my toes, one on each foot, when I removed my socks today. She said, yes, and not only did she go and get a needle, she offered to treat my blisters for me.

So there I was, sitting somewhere in Spain, with my sore feet propped up in a plastic lawn chair, and a girl from South Africa who

I met two days earlier is carefully doctoring my aching feet. One human being selflessly helping another. Very moving ...

As I say, we are in Villamayor del Rio, another oasis of sorts along our journey. I've covered right around 100 miles so far, and we have another 350 miles to go.

This day got off to quite an interesting start. We stayed last night at, well, at sort of a dump run by a very eccentric guy named Pedro. I don't want to say where this was exactly, because I think Pedro means well, but ... the albergue is in a very out-of-the-way location and is quite overpriced for what it is. However, breakfast is included in the fee, so Tom, Paula and I decided to go ahead and rest our weary bones there. After quickly showering, hand-washing our clothes and hanging them on the lines across the street behind the church, we head for the local bar-restaurant, where dinner is served at 8 o'clock. It is only about 3 o'clock when we get there, but we decided to wait it out, rather than return to our rather dilapidated sleeping quarters. Luckily, the bar has free Internet, so Paula and I take full advantage and spend several hours checking e-mail, blogging, updating Facebook pages and such. After a decent dinner of fried eggs, ham, peppers and the ever-present mound of french fries, Tom and I head back to the albergue about 9 o'clock to collect our laundry and get ready for lights out at 9:30. As we square away our things and get our backpacks ready for a quick exit in the morning, Paula arrives and tells us that Pedro had walked down to the bar and chased everyone back to the albergue for bedtime!

It was a comfortable and quiet night, and we all enjoyed a pretty good sleep, when WHAM! The lights in our room flashed on at 6 a.m., with Pedro standing there in an apron, announcing that it's time to get up and eat breakfast. "Es que hora para levantarse!" he says, or something like that.

"Jesus Christ," Paula says, sitting up in her bunk. Pedro leaves and I tell Tom to turn out the lights. He does, but here comes Pedro again, flipping back on the light. "No, no, no," he says, "El desayuno es en la mesa!" Good heavens. The last time anyone flipped on the lights

to roust me out of bed was my mama when I was a little kid. And the breakfast? One cup of so-so cafe con leche and some nearly burnt toast with butter and some kind of homemade marmalade.

Pedro did wave goodbye to us from a second-story window and bid us, "Buen Camino," as we left. Adios, dude ...

Paula left us behind today. She had seen signs for an albergue with a pool a few kilometers ahead of Villamayor del Rio, and decided she had to have a swim. Not a bad idea, but Tom and I didn't feel like walking another step, and so we told Paula to go on ahead, and we'd meet her in the morning at 8 o'clock. We missed out on the swim, but found our own oasis.

And I had an experience that proved one of the defining moments of my entire trip.

The albergue at Villamayor del Rio is a couple hundred meters off the Camino, down a two-lane blacktop road, and the friendly teen-aged daughter of the family who lived there greeted us and signed us up for a night's stay and a home-cooked dinner, complete with fresh vegetables from the garden. We were in a small, clean room with six or eight bunks, but only two other people were staying in it with us. It was always nice when the room was not full and crowded, people on top of each other, no room to move around, stretch out, relax. At the end of the long hallway were large, clean, new bathrooms. Nice place.

So we cleaned up, bought a couple cold cans of San Miguel, and headed for the backyard to wash clothes. To our surprise, we see Nix out there hanging up wet clothes to dry. Tom and I both thought that Ventosa was the last we would see of this smiling face from South Africa with the pierced bottom lip and roll-your-own cigarettes. Remember, it was Nix and Judy who saved the day awhile back by sharing with us what Tom and I called their magic South African pain pills.

If that were not kindness enough, Nix outdid herself this time when I asked if she had a needle I could borrow to drain a couple of small blisters on my toe. By now, I was paying attention – better late than never – to how people were taking care of their feet, and remembered how one effective treatment was to run a sterilized needle and thread through the blister, and leave the thread in place, to keep the fluids draining and prevent the blister from popping back up.

Nix said, sure, she had a needle, and even offered to take care of the blisters for me, if I'd like. Sure, I said, and she headed back inside to her room while Tom and I relaxed with cold beers in the shade of an umbrella-covered table and chairs.

She came right back with a needle, thread and some iodine. I propped my foot up in a white, plastic lawn chair and she set to work. It only took a few minutes, and I thanked her and she said no problem, and headed back inside. Now, I really didn't think much more about it as Tom and I relaxed and enjoyed the beautiful setting, but as time went on, it occurred to me that a pretty amazing thing had just happened. For Nix, who made her living then as a professional caregiver, it probably was no big deal, but to me, the idea that this woman from halfway across the world, whom I'd met just a few days before, had carefully popped blisters on my feet and medicated them for me was amazing. I'm not sure I would have done it.

I was extremely moved by it all. It was almost biblical. You know, the washing of feet and all that. And the more I thought about it, the more emotional I become. I went back inside the building and found Nix, sitting at a coin-operated computer, updating her Facebook or e-mailing or something, and I hugged her and thanked her again.

June 19

Ten days ago, I was scared and wanted very much to go home. Now, I never want this wonderful journey to end.

Today, I walked a little more than 17 kilometers through the most beautiful Spanish countryside, stopped and sat in the shade outside an old church in a tiny village called Villambista, where we ate sandwiches and watched the locals walk up the hill for 11 a.m. services, as the church bells rang across the cool morning. When we stood and began preparing to move on, I could hear singing from inside. The tall wooden doors were open and I wanted to walk over and look in, but somehow it seemed like an intrusion ...

We are staying today at a beautiful little albergue behind a hotel in Villafranca de Montes de Oca. I have no idea what all that means. However, it is a little town at the foot of the Montes de Oca that has been around since the 9th century. Tomorrow, we will pass through San Juan de Ortega and be on the road to the city of Burgos, leaving "only" 316 miles to Santiago.

I am still traveling with Tom and Paula, although I felt the urge early this morning to strike out on my own. I am understanding now what the South African girl, Verity, was talking about when she explained the Camino as a metaphor for life and renewal.

If the beginning stages of the Camino are like the birth and onset of early childhood, filled with doubts, fears, growing pains, etc., I have surely experienced those things since I arrived in Pamplona. And I wondered as I walked this morning whether babies become terrified as the birth process begins. Do they understand what is happening, and are they afraid to leave the safety and warmth of their mother? And what effect does this trauma have on them? Do the very secure, confident individuals among us somehow recover from that better than others? Does anyone fully recover from it?

And now that I am finding my footing and feeling more confident, I think I am starting to feel that maybe I need to break away from the safety and security that my new friends have helped me find. For two days in the beginning, I walked alone and felt mostly OK, but since then we have traveled most of the time together, sometimes separating for kilometers at a time as someone slowed down a bit, someone else maybe picked up the pace a little, but always coming back together at some point.

One of these days soon, I will leave and venture out on my own again, because I think I need to. But I am torn. I want to test myself some more, see what I can find and learn on my own, but I do not want to leave my new friends. I am not scared any more, but the three of us have become close over the past week or so, and I enjoy their company so much. I will miss them when the time comes to go ...

Villafranca was another very nice albergue, adjacent to what appeared to be a pretty luxurious hotel, and it was new and clean and completely comfortable. Tom and I walked down the street to a tienda and bought groceries for dinner

– bread, cheese, sausage, wine, some asparagus, a can of olives, some other stuff – and ate in the albergue's little kitchen, overlooking the countryside and the ever-present church.

We stayed that night in a room with six or eight bunk beds. Tom and I were closest to the door, me on the top bunk and him on the bottom, and a woman from Canada and her teenage daughter were over by the far wall. Other people were in-between, but I can't remember now who they were, or if we even knew them.

Sometime in the middle of the night, I was awakened by the Canadian woman shaking me by the shoulder.

"You're snoring," she said.

Groggily, I rolled over and heard Tom sawing some pretty impressive logs underneath me, and I said to the woman, "I think it's Tom."

"It's both of you," she said, exasperatedly, "in symphony!"

Snoring was one of the things I was warned about during my research, and my chats on the Internet Camino forum. Bringing earplugs is highly recommended, if you're any kind of light sleeper, or sensitive to noise in the night. I wake up if the wind blows too loudly outside, so I definitely heeded that advice, and didn't really have any serious sleeping problems at all. In fact, I slept pretty well, actually. But this time, I was apparently the one causing problems.

We saw that woman and her daughter again on down the road, but they never slept in the same room with us again. Whether that was by coincidence or by design, I'm not sure.

Nevertheless, we headed out early the next day, climbing a path illuminated only by our flashlights in the cool, early morning darkness. Going up, up, up … suddenly, off to the right, there is Karl, the big, bearded German, sitting cross-legged in the tall grass, facing east, waiting for the sunrise. He says he is going to take some pictures.

We continue on, until we reach our first stop at San Juan de Ortega, where we have a very good café con leche and snacks at a bar on the plaza outside the centuries-old monastery. Inside the chapel is incredible artwork and sculpture that goes back as far as 1462. Also on display is the stone sarcophagus of San Juan, containing the remains of the man who was known for building bridges, hospitals, churches and hostels throughout the region to serve Camino pilgrims.

It was an arduous 12.2-kilometer ascent this morning that included lovely shaded, winding stretches through thick forests, with tall pines and fir trees. At one point, Paula turned to me and said merrily, "Look, a forest of Christmas trees!" Then she broke out into a rendition of the classic song, "O' Christmas Tree."

So, we sat for awhile on the plaza and rested our feet. I took off my shoes and socks, walking gingerly around in my flip-flops. By now, I've learned to let my feet and socks dry out every now and then, maybe change socks. I take a few pictures of my damaged feet for posterity.

Then it was on to Villambista, where Tom and I decide to sit for awhile on a bench in the shade outside an old, stone church building. We watch as an elderly lady – she's got to be at least in her 70s, maybe 80s – slowly makes her way toward the tall wooden door on the side, grabs the door handle, leans her shoulder into it and bangs the door open with her hip. She has obviously done this before. Then she goes on inside.

Tom reminds me that we have sandwiches that Nix gave us last night. After dinner, she whipped out a loaf of crusty bread, some ham, a tomato and made a batch of little sandwiches for her and Judy's lunch the next day. She offered us a couple and we were happy to accept. They were fantastic, and even had some mayonnaise on them. Delicious. Mayonnaise and mustard and such are not included with traditional Spanish boccadillos (sandwiches). Not the ones I've had so far, anyway.

So we ate and rested and watched as about a dozen people came up the hill for morning services as bells rang across the morning. A small car arrived with what we presumed was the traveling minister, a tall, young, dark-haired guy wearing a Bruce Springsteen tee shirt. He was the only young person, and everybody else was old enough to be his grandparents, at least, so we figured he must be the minister.

June 21

*W*hat an amazing day. After lacing up my hiking shoes and heading off to find a nice cafe con leche, I began to notice something strange. Something missing.

Pain in my left foot.

For the first time in more than a week, I´m walking without pain! What a feeling! Birds are circling in the cool morning air, against a clear blue sky, and it feels normal to walk again. No gingerly stepping with the left foot. No limping. No aching and throbbing. I´d almost forgotten what it feels like. Since that massive blister ballooned on the bottom of my foot seven or eight days ago, right on the pad where you put your weight when you step, it´s been kind of a struggle. Finally, it seems to be healing. How great is that? Oh, and by the way, the cafe con leche was excellent, and the sugary, cinnamony apple pastry was even better.

Today, we arrived at Burgos and visited its famous 13th century cathedral. Words can´t do the place justice, so I won´t even bother trying to describe it. It is truly incredible. Google it, folks, and check it out. We´re staying in the big, municipal albergue here, directly behind the cathedral. Pretty nice place. Five floors, clean and roomy. Only 4 euros for the night. Coin-operated Internet.

We had an incredible evening yesterday in a little place called Atapuerca. This is the site of the discovery of the oldest human remains in Europe, dating back over 900,000 years. That's not the incredible part, though.

The day began before first light, as we headed out of Villafranca, with the path illuminated only by our flashlights. An arduous 12-kilometer climb. Up, up, up. Suddenly, off to the right, I see Karl, the big, bearded German, sitting cross-legged in the tall grass, waiting for the sun to rise over the distant mountains. This is the guy who wished me, "Goode night, Texas Ranger," the other night. Amazing guy. This is his second Camino, and he has plans to take a year off from work, and to go live in a commune somewhere in southern Spain, I think it is. When he caught up with us later in San Juan de Ortega, he showed us some beautiful photos he took of the sunrise.

It was a tough, painful climb to San Juan — which also has a lovely medieval church that contains artwork and sculpture dating back to 1462 — but included hikes through beautiful forests of tall pines and fir trees. "Look," Paula said, at one point, "it's a forest of Christmas trees," before breaking out in a rendition of the song, Ó Christmas Tree.

We eventually got to a nice little albergue in Atapuerca, claimed beds, showered, washed the day's clothes, rested, shopped for dinner at the local tienda and cooked a great spaghetti dinner in the albergue kitchen. OK, Tom cooked and I supervised. Later is when the really incredible stuff happened.

As we sat out on the patio late in the evening, Paula broke out her new ukelele, starting plinking around on it, and began attracting an audience. Before long, there were six of us: Paula, Tom, me, a French guy named Didier, a German guy named Otto, and another German guy named Paul. Before it was all over, the six of us were laughing and talking, sharing a bottle of wine, and singing the reggae song, "Don't Worry; Be Happy." Never in my wildest dreams. Amazing ...

Magnificent 13th century Catedral de Santa Maria at
Burgos, one of the larger cities along the Camino

Musicians outside Burgos cathedral

What an amazing day it was. When I got here, I was so uncomfortable, so scared, so unsure of myself. I never imagined that I would be sitting in the middle of nowhere in Spain – Spain! – talking and laughing and singing with people from England, France, Norway, Germany, Italy, South Africa, Holland. And such wonderful people. So warm and kind and loving.

It made me think that when you get down to it, the world is actually a pretty nice place. It's really not, of course. The world is a pretty screwed-up place, a dangerous place, and can be a scary place. Nix and Judy talked about the muggings, robberies, carjackings and such that are so commonplace back home in their native Cape Town. You don't wear jewelry when you go out, they said, or someone will take it from you. Simple as that. You will be mugged.

Just a fact of life where they live. And Tom, who has lived in a number of different countries, talking about how violence in many parts of the world is more the rule than the exception. I had no idea. I've never been exposed to anything like that.

I grew up in Houston, Texas, a large, somewhat dangerous city, but the only crime I ever really experienced was someone stealing a stereo and speakers out of my new pickup truck at an apartment complex, and having a pistol waved in my face when I inadvertently walked in on a late-night armed robbery at a pizza restaurant. Well, there was the time when a friend and I got jumped and beat up by a gang of drunk teenagers outside a high school dance in Spring Branch. And the time my girlfriend and I were accosted at Hermann Park by a group of self-medicated assholes. I was at a party once when a pretty serious argument broke out over some drug deal and the host went into his bedroom and came back with a large revolver and sat down on the couch, pistol on his lap. I guess there were scary moments, but the world I grew up in, you never really felt unsafe. Nothing like what they described.

And that's the way it was on the Camino. I never felt any kind of danger, walking alone through the countryside. Walking alone through Logrono or Burgos or the other larger cities we passed through. I never came close to feeling any kind of danger, or apprehension about safety. It was like a different world. Like stepping back in time. A simpler time. A friendlier time.

It was sort of like being in a movie or something. Paula probably said it best when she said (and you have to imagine this being said in a sort of melodic British accent), "It's like stepping into an oil painting." And it was. It was like a fantasy. A wonderful real-life fantasy.

Anyway, we waited and waited outside the albergue this morning in Atapuerca for Paula. She has proven to be quite the slow-starter in the morning, and this time Tom loses a little patience and gets tired of waiting. She will catch up with us later, he says, let's go, and we head over to the local tienda for coffee and some breakfast.

It's an absolutely beautiful day, and as we head up the street, carrying our backpacks and trekking poles, I notice after a couple of minutes that my foot does not hurt. I'm walking along as usual, when all of a sudden, I realize that something is different. When I step down onto my left foot, there is no pain. No more pain! It feels strange. Like something is missing. It actually takes me a moment to understand what is happening. I have gotten so used to the pain being there, a constant companion for a week or so, and now it is gone. Completely gone. It still feels like I'm stepping on something every other step, like there's something stuck to the bottom of my foot, or maybe something in my shoe, but it does not hurt.

It is amazing how good and normal it feels to walk now. I tell Tom about it, but I don't want to celebrate too much, since he is still in quite a lot of pain. At some point later on down the road, I tell him that I really don't know how I endured so much pain for so long, walking for hours and hours each day on an extremely angry foot. How did I do it? How did I manage? The pain pills helped, of course, but that only dulled the agony and made it somewhat bearable. Imagine walking for hours on end, day after day, with a foot throbbing and screaming in pain every time you set it down.

Tom, who is a retired mechanical engineer and a pretty brilliant guy, explained that pain is mostly a nuisance. I could not remember, of course, exactly what he said word-for-word, but it was very logical and quite profound, and I wanted to repeat it here, so I asked him a few months later in an e-mail if he could remember what it was that he told me that day.

"Let's see if I can give a clear thought on pain," he wrote. *"Pain in itself is just a flashing light and of no importance. When one feels pain, it is because our body is sending a message that something is not quite as it should be. Our reaction to this is to try to establish what the problem is. The next thing is to decide to remedy what is wrong, if possible.*

"A broken leg stops us from walking, not because it hurts, but because it is impossible mechanically to do so. If we discover that the pain is indicating something not very serious (blisters, for example), we can decide to carry on in spite of it. If we do so, I find that the pain seems to subside in intensity with time. I think the subconscious tells the nervous system to stop sending signals because it's not going to take any notice, so the pain gradually decreases. This is the engineer's answer to the question – a philosopher might say the same with very different words."

Nevertheless, pain or no pain, it was a pretty rugged walk that day into Burgos, a city of about 200,000. A lot of the path was uphill and rocky, a dirt trail littered with rocks of all shapes and sizes, requiring careful stepping and deliberate movements. Finally, we reached the top of the hill and saw the city stretched out before us, far in the distance, with the Camino path winding its way ahead. There was a long way to go, and we pressed on.

When we get to the outskirts of the city, we decide that we will take a bus to the city centre, rather than walk a couple more miles through heavy traffic along busy streets. A young boy, probably about 13-14 years old, stops on his bicycle to drink out of a fountain, and Tom asks him in Spanish about catching a bus. The boy says he doesn't know, but we manage to find a nice bar just down the road, and they tell us inside that the next bus will be along in such-and-such, and there is a bus stop just outside. We have a cold beer and something to eat, then catch the next bus to the cathedral downtown.

The bus lets us off a few blocks from the cathedral, the Catedral de Santa Maria, and we head there to check it out. A couple of dreadlocked dudes are playing some pretty cool Eastern-style music inside a large covered archway on one side, on some bongos and another instrument I cannot name, and we head on in and pay the admission fee, along with another euro to store our backpacks in a locker. The cathedral is magnificent, unbelievable. Never seen anything like it. The place is massive, and completely beautiful. Hard to describe, really.

It is one of the largest cathedrals in Spain, and consists of a number of different architectural styles, as additions were made over the centuries to the original structure, but essentially it is described as Gothic, with tall spires reaching for the sky, and a breathtaking array of gold and sculpture and paintings inside.

We wander around for awhile, taking pictures and just basically being amazed at the beauty. After we have our fill, we retrieve our backpacks and head to the nearby albergue, just off the cathedral square. It's one of those huge, multi-floor monstrosities, and we register at the front desk, then leave our shoes in this gigantic pull-out shoe closet, and take the elevator up to our assigned beds. I take the top bunk and notice right away that it appears to be stained with – I don't know what it is – some sort of disgusting-looking brown stains all over the dingy sheet. Blood maybe? I go back downstairs and explain the best I can that the sheet is really dirty and can I get a new one.

One of the people downstairs comes up and takes a look, and immediately goes and gets a new sheet, and puts it on the bed for me. Cool. Problem solved. I take a shower and change clothes, then head down to the large lounge area and buy a can of San Miguel from one of the vending machines. I'd read about the vending machines here that sell beer, but this is the first one I've come across.

The place is busy, busy, and crowded with Camino bicyclists who park their bikes in a designated area between the check-in desk and the lounge. We saw a lot of bicyclists on the Camino, and some of the places they had to traverse had to have been difficult. Some of the inclines, and the places where even walking was difficult, across rocks and over streams. I could not imagine pedaling such places.

One interesting thing I noticed about the bicyclists was the age disparity in a number of the groups. Guys probably in their 20s, riding with men in their 40s, 50s, maybe even 60s. There doesn't appear to be the age discrimination here that one so often finds in the U.S. Young guys hanging out with the old farts, and it's no big deal.

Meanwhile, down in the albergue lounge area, there are vending machines, a dozen or so tables to sit at, and several computers with the usual coin-operated Internet access. As far as large municipal albergues go, it's not a bad place. Modern, clean and fairly comfortable. Again, it's amazing to me to think about the fact that here I am, laying on the top bunk on the third level of a five-floor, restored 16th-century building in Spain, with people from all over the world – all over the world – walking around, showering and sleeping, in the same place.

Paula is in here somewhere, and I saw Didier awhile ago. I suspect Paul is here, too, and I even saw Otto earlier. There's a girl from Boston named Jaime whom I met and talked with for awhile outside. And a young kid from Germany. How weird is that? All these people, on the same journey, headed to the same place.

The beds are separated by cubicles into groups of four, and our bunks are on the end. When I go to take my shower, I see people in the other bunks, some reading, some just relaxing. The bathrooms and showers are nearby, and the only real problem comes when it's time for lights out. The lights go out at 10 p.m., and I'm ready for sleep, but our beds are near the doorway that leads to the elevator, and there's a lot of noise coming from there. People talking, talking, talking. One of the primary culprits is this very eccentric, moustachioed artist from Holland, who is loudly talking to someone just outside the dormitory doors. C'mon, dude, go to bed already.

June 23

T oday, we walked a fairly easy 20 kilometers into Castrojeriz, where we checked into the municipal albergue, and will spend the night on mattresses on the floor of a small gymnasium. Aches and pains are minimal today, as the famous blister has pretty much healed. However, I did manage to jar my back a little bit this morning when I decided to jump down about three feet from one path to another, with my backpack on. Turned out to be not such a good idea. No major damage, but I won't be jumping any more for awhile.

The past two days have been good for learning Camino lessons. Yesterday started out sort of a blech day – not good, not bad. Just sort of slogging our way out of Burgos, a long haul from the city centre and onto the meseta, the long, dry, rolling plains that mark the middle section of the Camino. We seem to have left Paula behind now, so Tom and I carry on through the rolling wheat fields, neither of us particularly enthusiastic about walking this day. The albergue was comfortable and the sleeping OK, but there seems to be something about the large cities that is tiring, a different energy than when we are out in the country.

After about 10 kilometers or so, we stop for a cafe con leche in a little town called Tardajos. Sitting under umbrellas at the local bar/cafe, sipping a steaming café con leche, I hear a voice behind me that sounds exactly like John Lennon. I'm probably looking for something – anything – to provide a boost for the day, so I turn and say, "You sound just like John Lennon." And that´s how we met Nick, a 33-year-old world traveler and world-class character from Manchester, England.

When he works, Nick is a tour guide, so he is quite the talker, which we find out during the next 10 kilometers to Hornillos del Camino.

I walked alone with Nick for several kilometers – while Tom walked up ahead a few meters with Nick's partner, Carlos of Miami – and we talked about all kinds of things: politics, religion, music. Nick is a master of the quip: "If it weren´t for the pickpockets and the frisking at the airports, I wouldn´t have a sex life at all." His travels have taken him all over the world, and this guy has a pretty good and unique outlook. He says institutionalized religion has ruined things for a lot of people, and I agree. Churches and their leaders have complicated things and made a lot of arbitrary rules that really have nothing to do with Jesus´ fairly simple message about how to behave.

Nick said one thing that impressed him about the Bible story is the part about Jesus hanging on the cross, and saying, "Father, why hast thou forsaken me?" According to Nick, that showed his humanness and frailty, perhaps even an imperfection that demonstrates that it is OK to not be perfect. And that even though he is not perfect and never will be, that does not mean he is flawed, but only that he is human. And that he therefore can love himself.

That´s the main thing I took from my time with ol´ Nick – what it means to love oneself. I´ve always thought that sounded kinda weird and arrogant: "I love myself." To me, that always sounded like I would be saying, "I´m the greatest thing on Earth." But that´s not it. It´s more that you can accept yourself for who and what you are, warts and all. And if you don´t intentionally set out to harm other people, and try to follow Jesus´ extremely simple message of loving your brother as yourself, then you´re a pretty good bloke. And you should love yourself. Maybe I can learn to do that.

Anyway, so Nick lifted our spirits and taught me something, even as he was wearing out our eardrums with his non-stop chatter. Oh, yeah, he also taught us something about traveling light. We stopped at one point to take on water, and I walked over and picked up Nick's small backpack. The thing couldn't have weighed more than 10 pounds! Hell, my cargo shorts weigh nearly that much, with all the crap stuffed in the pockets. He picks up my backpack, and his eyes get big. "What have ya got in here, a couple of bricks in case you need to build a barbecue?"

The last we saw of Nick, he had just dunked his head in a city fountain in Hornillos del Camino, plopped his straw hat back on his head, and headed off shirtless onto the meseta to catch up with Carlos. We'd had enough for the day and were checking into the municipal albergue.

That chance meeting, though, brought to fruition something I told Tom earlier in the day, as we stopped just outside Burgos to have a sit and eat an orange. It was starting out to be a not-so-good day, but I decided that I would keep putting one foot in front of the other, and wait for that one bright spot in the day that would turn things around. And sure enough, it happened.

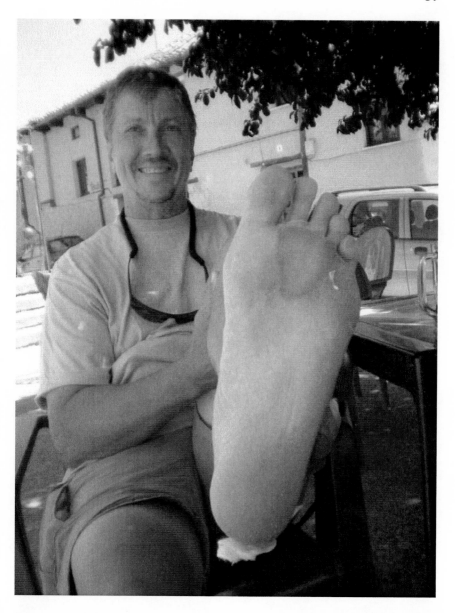

Happy that my severely blistered foot is finally healing

Today was just one example of lessons learned on the Camino. Many of those lessons have involved very simple things. Things that other people learn and absorb and are able to live by quite naturally. Things like gratitude. Trust. Patience. Hope. Optimism.

June 24

O K, folks, I'm sitting at a little rest area with concrete picnic tables, eating a platano (banana) and wearing long pants, t-shirt and pullover fleece jacket. It's cold! I'm pretty sure there is no chilly breeze to be found anywhere in Texas right now. More later ...

Tom and I take a breather somewhere on the Camino

Last night was the albergue from hell in a place called Castrojeriz. It's a nice, pretty, hilly little town of about 1,000 people with some sort of all-night summer solstice festival going on, but the municipal albergue turned out to be a nightmare.

I guess we arrived a little late in the afternoon and all the bunks were already occupied, so we got mattresses on the floor of what appears to be a small gymnasium. The guy who ran the place was nice and a real character, an old Spanish hippie, I suspect, and the co-ed bathrooms are large and clean, so we shower and change and wash our clothes in the sink, hang them out to dry, then go out and find a bar where we sit and have an ice cold beer – so damn good after a long day's walk – then buy a six-pack to go. We head back to the albergue, which sits high atop a long set of concrete steps, and sit out on the patio, watching the festivities down on the street below. There is music and some sort of parade and festival queen, and then they all march out of sight, apparently to party around a big bonfire somewhere.

Eventually, we head inside to get ready for sleep. A lot of people in the bunks are already down for the night, and I try not to make too much noise as I walk back and forth to the bathroom across the creaky, wooden gym floor. Too bad other people did not try and extend the same courtesy later.

The mattresses were fine and comfortable, and it was another pretty good night's sleep, but at 5 o'clock in the morning, it was bedlam. Dozens of people started rolling out of their bunks, stomping around, shining flashlights all over the place, talking loudly with no regard for the people who were not ready to get up just yet. Over in the bathroom-shower area, nobody bothers to keep the door closed, so the bright lights from in there are shining across the room and its sounds like there is a damn convention going on.

Nevertheless, we head out about 7 a.m. for another planned 20-kilometer day. Shortly after leaving Castrojeriz, we start climbing. According to the guidebook, it's only about a 100-meter increase in elevation over about a 2-3 kilometer distance, but it sure ain't no walk in the park, either.

After the climb, though, the path heads blessedly downhill and onward through the meseta. The morning goes smoothly and we stop for a break and a snack at Itero de la Vega, home of a beautiful 16th century church, before pressing on to our destination for the day at Boadilla del Camino, home of yet another 16th century church.

It was the last eight kilometers when the day turned a little ugly. My back, slightly tweaked from yesterday's ill-advised leap of stupidity, was now seriously hurting. Alf and Anita, a couple from Norway who were walking a short distance behind me, later confirmed my suspicions that I was listing badly to the right as I trudged along. Jytte was just ahead of me, and she was concerned enough that she asked me twice to let her carry my backpack for me. My ego wouldn't let me agree to that, so I struggled along.

The last two kilometers were almost unbearable, until we finally reached an oasis at the En El Camino albergue. The people were incredibly warm and inviting, and the backyard is a sight to see. Situated between the main house and the dormitory (a beautifully converted barn), there is a swimming pool surrounded by a large, manicured lawn, tall shade trees and flowers everywhere. From most areas of the yard, you can see the bell tower of the ancient Iglesia Santa Maria. Inside the church is a stunning 14th century stone baptismal font, illuminated softly by afternoon sunlight streaming through the window.

We decide we may stay here an extra day. Tom's feet have become a serious problem, and he is feeling really discouraged. My back is killing me, and we're thinking that a day's rest may be just what the doctor ordered, so to speak.

After showering and washing clothes and tending to the usual duties at day's end, I head over to the main house and sit under an umbrella on the patio and order a tall cerveza, and a bowl of garlic soup. Never had garlic soup before, and it is delicious. A dozen or so other people are sitting around, talking and drinking and eating. Some are dipping their feet into the pool, while others are swimming. This place is fantastic.

I decide to go try and lay down for awhile. Maybe my back will feel better. I try and sleep a little, but can't, so I go up for another beer and write for awhile in my journal. As Jytte and I made our way here earlier, we were talking about foot rubs, and as I sat in the lounge area of the dorm, she came in and asked me if I wanted that foot massage. Most definitely, I said.

So she pulled up a chair, whipped out a bottle of lotion and put my feet in her lap. Not only did she massage and rub my sore feet with her lotioned hands, she held each foot by the heel with one hand and by the toes with the other. Carefully, she pushed and pulled and twisted and turned, pausing at times in concentration, then pushing and pulling, twisting and turning some more. I could actually feel the manipulations all the way up in my lower back. I don't know exactly how long it took, but when she finished and I got up and walked around, my back felt good. Really good.

Two hours earlier, I could hardly walk and now I am OK. Amazing.

We had a fine three-course community dinner that night, with our hosts serving us more garlic soup, grilled fish, wine and dessert. A room full of people from all over the world, eating together, talking and laughing.

June 25

*P*ain and sadness.
  It was a day for both.

*Two or three days ago, I took an ill-advised leap of stupidity —
jumping about three feet down from one path to another with 20 pounds
strapped to my back — and yesterday I paid for it. At first, it seemed
like no big deal, but by midday Friday, I was a mess. Practically
staggering the last two kilometers into Boadilla del Camino, I finally
made it to the albergue, where I was greeted on a beautifully manicured
lawn by a pretty, smiling, dark-haired Italian girl, "You want to sleep
here?" Very much, yes, I do ...*

*I sat for awhile and rested, then went to the bar and ate a bowl of
garlic soup — it's really good stuff, y'all — and went to the bunkhouse
to lay down. Before dinner, one of my new friends, Jytte (Yitta) of
Denmark, massaged and manipulated my feet, pushing, pulling,
rubbing, turning, twisting. It felt really good and I could feel it in my
lower back when she pushed and pulled. Apparently, though, the pain
dislodged and traveled upward into my heart and my head. It was only
a short time later that I became very sad and homesick. I missed my
family and felt lonely again.*

*After dinner, Jytte and I talked for awhile and I felt a little better.
Pain — physical or emotional — is a powerful thing, isn't it? Hard to
ignore. Hard to get rid of. But I shed a few tears and felt a little lighter*

*as we walked through the village, past the historic Iglesia Santa Marie.
I had a good night's sleep and now – sitting outside a bar in Fromista,
drinking cafe con leche and eating a tortilla y patata – I feel pretty good.
It was a quick and easy 6-kilometer walk here this morning, and Tom
and Jytte arrived a few minutes after I did. In a few minutes more, we
will head out again toward Carrion de los Condes ...*

**Me, Jytte and Tom relaxing outside an albergue after a
good day's walk**

My eyes have been opened quite a bit on this journey, and
I truly believe that the pain was somehow coaxed out of my
back by Jytte's manipulations, but then got lodged in my
heart. Not a physical pain in my heart, but an emotional pain.
And are the two kinds really so different?

While my back now felt remarkably back to normal, I was
nearly overcome with sadness, and a feeling of homesickness
that I had not experienced since I got here. After dinner,

which buoyed my spirits a little bit, the kindness and fellowship with so many like-minded people sharing such an incredible adventure, Jytte and I walked out of the albergue and past the Iglesia Santa Maria, around a few old buildings and out to a grassy area beside a fence, past a young Spanish guy and gal who appeared to be doing some sort of yoga. Jytte had me lay down in the grass and close my eyes, and she lay down beside me, talking in a quiet voice, doing a sort of hypnosis treatment in which you are to visualize various colors, see the colors in your mind, concentrate on them and let them fill your heart. I've experienced this sort of hypnosis before, but I can't really explain how it works. A lot of it is about colors, and visualization. It is a form of energy healing that is designed to remove negativity from your body and open your heart to loving and healing energy.

Sounds like a lot of hocus-pocus maybe, but the truth is that it really can work. After I underwent some hypnosis sessions a number of years ago to try and improve my golf game, I learned about things like reflexology, meditation, chakras and Reiki, even taking classes and becoming a certified Reiki practitioner.

One time a few years ago, I took advantage of an offer for a free 30-minute Reiki treatment at a place near my home. I stretched out on a massage table, and several people placed their hands on various parts of my body: my head, neck, shoulders, back, feet, calves, arms, hands. Just placed their hands there in silence, moving to different areas as they felt led to do so, transferring positive energy from the universe through their bodies into mine.

When they finished, I felt much like I do at the end of a traditional, hour-long massage treatment. Totally relaxed, peaceful, de-stressed. Wonderful. And I also felt quite humble, and surrounded with love. I hugged the people who had treated me, and they hugged me back. Complete strangers who had volunteered their time and talents to help me. It was pretty remarkable.

Unfortunately, the session with Jytte was not as successful, and she told me that she could feel me blocking her energy from reaching into my heart. I understood what she meant, and I believed her. I tried to let go, but I couldn't. I am very protective of my heart. My heart has been broken, truly broken, and it is the worst kind of pain I have ever felt. So it is difficult for me to leave my heart unguarded.

But I did manage to shed a few tears after I sat up and we continued to talk. The tears were unusual for me, and cathartic. It felt good to cry, and I felt a little better. Crying does not come easily for me, and I know the reason why. Part of it stems from the way I was raised, and part of it comes from the death of my mother.

My mother, Billie Jo Clark, was a hard-working, fun-loving, creative, wonderful woman. She was the one person in my life who I always knew loved me. I always trusted that, and never doubted it. It was something I could always count on. No matter what, I knew my mother loved me, unconditionally. It was only after she died that I realized she was not perfect, and that she was in fact a flawed human being, just like everyone else. But I always knew she loved me. My father's love, on the other hand, I never really felt. It seemed more like something to be earned, and I never could seem to earn it, no matter how hard I tried.

And when my mother died, I was kind of numb. I think I was numb and mostly in denial from the day my sister called me and said that doctors had found "a mass" in our mother's brain. I had never even considered my mother dying. I'd experienced people dying before – my two grandfathers (one by suicide), one of my grandmothers, a kid from church hit by a car when I was about nine years old, a teenage friend in a car wreck – but not my mother.

And even as she bravely battled her brain cancer for more than a year, I never really considered the finality of her being gone forever. Never seeing her again. Never hearing her voice again. Never feeling her embrace. I just wouldn't let myself imagine it. I couldn't imagine it.

At her memorial service, at a little church in the woods near her home in Iola, Texas, I walked into the chapel and saw a little table filled with photographs. That's when it really hit me. My mother was not there. Only pictures of her. My sister, brother and I stood and spoke about our mother, one at a time. I had written a one-page eulogy of sorts, sort of a tribute or obituary, I guess, and when I found out that I was expected to speak at the service, I decided I would read that. When I walked up the podium, and looked out at the hundred or so people who were there, I could not speak. Her name was to be the first thing I said, that was the way I had written it, and the words would not come. I could feel the floodgate in my throat straining, as the emotion threatened to overwhelm me, if I dared try to talk.

I stood up there for at least five minutes, with my head down, staring at the piece of paper, swallowing hard and trying to compose myself. Finally, I managed to push everything down, down, down, and I was able to say her name out loud and read the essay about my mother's life without breaking down. My voice was choked, but I did not cry. I thought if I started crying, I might never stop.

That was in June 2000, and I really haven't cried since. Well, I have shed a tear or two a couple of times, but never that full-force, tears-running-down-your-face kind of crying that is so good for releasing emotions. I just can't do it. Mostly, at really sad movies and when I think of certain things, I get that choked-up feeling where your throat hurts, but the tears just won't come.

I did cry a little bit that afternoon in front of Jytte, though – maybe 6 or 8 actual tears spilled out – and I have to admit that it felt really good. Jytte is a pretty wise person, in her own way, and she told me that pain is not something to be feared or avoided. It is a positive thing, a temporary thing, and a signal that something important needs attention.

"Every pain has a meaning," she said, *"and when you find the meaning, you don't need the pain anymore."*

As the sun began to set, we got up and walked back past the young couple doing yoga poses in the grass, and alongside the Iglesia Santa Maria, and back to the albergue for sleep.

June 27

I took off this morning from the monastery in the early morning hours, set to begin the difficult 17-kilometer slog across the hot and dry meseta. Wouldn't ya know it, there's a heat wave going on right now all across Spain! The going was cool for the first couple hours, and I plopped down in the grass beside the path to rest for awhile, and let my feet and socks dry out some. About 20 minutes later, here comes good ol' Tom, and a few minutes after that is Jytte.

They decide to join me but Tom is a bit reluctant to have a sit. "If I sit down, I don't know if I'll be able to get back up," he says. Jytte tells him we will help him get up when the time comes, if he needs us to. So Tom sits and we all have a snack and rest. After awhile, Jytte says to Tom, "You about ready to get up?" Here comes the quote of the day ...

In his refined British accent, Tom slowly answers: "I'm preparing for it."

Something I haven't talked about thus far is one of the somewhat unpleasant but necessary realities of the Camino. One very helpful hint I picked up on the Camino de Santiago chat forum that helped me prepare for my trip was the suggestion to include an emergency roll of toilet paper in the backpack. I think the Europeans refer to it as a "loo roll."

To save space, you slide the cardboard tube out from the middle of the roll, then smash the roll flat and stick it in your backpack. So that's what I did.

It didn't take long for this to come in very handy. I think it may have been the first day, actually. Maybe the second day. I was walking by myself past a large olive grove early in the morning when a certain familiar urgency started percolating in my bowels. Oh, no, you've got to be kidding, I thought. I was completely out in the middle of nowhere, and I knew from experience that this was not going to go away. There were several people walking a short distance behind me – I could hear their voices back there – so I started looking for a detour that might offer some privacy.

I found a likely-looking place and stepped off the path, headed a few meters up into the orchard and discovered that others had been there before me. Little piles of toilet paper surrounded one of the low-growing trees. Ha! Guess I'm not the only one. So I dropped my backpack, found my loo roll, dropped my cargo shorts and carefully squatted behind the olive tree. Sweet relief.

And this was not the only time this happened.

Remember, little things become very important out here on the Camino, and there was the day when I found myself facing another bathroom emergency, far from civilization, and I walked around behind an old storage building or something beside the path, into a wooded area, and found clear-cut signs of another apparently popular dumping ground.

Not only was it a place hidden from sight of the Camino, but there also was a large tree branch on the ground that provided a perfect, very comfortable seat to answer nature's call. It was the highlight of my day. I sat on the log and did my business.

And I told Tom and Jytte about it later. I really did, because I thought it was very cool. Finding a comfortable place to have an emergency sit and relieve myself. It was actually very nice. One of those unexpected moments, like finding some fruit in your backpack that you didn't know was there. Well, not exactly like that, but you know what I mean. I prefaced my story by telling them it was "disgusting" when I retold the tale, and Jytte said, "Why is that disgusting?" Gotta love her.

And the time came again today for such an emergency. It was one of the reasons I stopped where I did, in front of somebody's cattle shed or something, off to the right of the Camino. There was a big metal gate and it was fenced off with barbed wire, so there was no going in there. I dropped my backpack, grabbed my loo roll and searched for a secure location. Over here? No. Over there? Not good. Finally I found a place, down and across a small ditch, behind some trees.

Then I went back and unpacked my sleeping bag cover, stretched it out on the grass beside the path, took off my shoes and relaxed for awhile. People passed by from time to time, some not noticing me laying there, others offering "Buen Camino" as they walked along. Then Tom and Jytte appeared, sat down and rested for awhile, and Tom provided us with the quote of the day and a good laugh.

We carried on together and arrived before too long at Calzadilla de la Cueza, described in the guidebook as "a typical Camino village with a central street that forms the Way itself." It's hot and dry and dusty, and even though it's still early in the day, we decide to stop. There's no one at the albergue to check us in for the night, but another pilgrim who is already there says that we should go ahead and claim our beds, and the hospitalera will be back shortly. Here's what I wrote in my journal:

I've spent most of the day hangin' around the albergue here in Calzadilla. Pretty bored, actually. My damn blog got suspended for some reason, and that bugs the shit out of me. I can't imagine they won't reactivate it, but I'd hate to lose all the stuff I've written so far. I'm kind of planned to use the blog stuff as the basis for a book. Everything is probably in the journal, too, but ...

This town is not the most exciting place in the world. I don't know what it's all about, but basically there's nothing here. An albergue – fairly nice, with a pool out back – a bar/restaurant just down the road, a bunch of dilapidated buildings, and that's about it. There are three old men sitting beside me outside the bar, talking about who-knows-what. My verbal comprehension skills in Spanish are not so good, so I can only catch bits and pieces of what they're saying. I can't translate in my mind fast enough to keep up.

I'm feeling kind of shitty right now, to tell the truth. Two reasons I can come up with: one, my blog being suspended; two, I'm tired of walking only half a day, then stopping. After you shower, wash your clothes, and hang 'em up, there's nothing else to do. I'm fucking bored.

Jytte and I talk about it at some point during the afternoon, and she feels the same way. We know Tom has been struggling and we don't want to leave him behind, but we also don't want to sit around all afternoon any more. We want to walk. It's becoming sort of a dilemma.

Then, we are both surprised and relieved later in the evening when Tom brings up the same thing. He, too, was bored out of his skull this afternoon and thinks we should have walked some more today. It was a big relief to hear him say that.

Jytte, who is sort of a bundle of nervous energy, takes off to explore the local church. Tom stretches out for a nap, and I lay in my bunk for awhile, but I'm not tired. So I get up, put my shoes on and head up to the bar for another beer and another hour on the Internet.

We all have dinner that night at the restaurant inside the bar, and like everywhere else here, it is very elegant and nice. We're in a dusty little podunk farming town, out in the middle of nowhere, and the little restaurant is like a fine dining experience, with the linen tablecloths and napkins, china saucers and plates and bowls, gleaming silverware. The hospitalera from the albergue walks in and joins us, and we talked a lot about spirituality and healing. She is some sort of healer, but speaks with a thick Eastern European accent, so it's a little hard to understand everything she says. There is a lot of smiling and nodding. Something about this woman rubs Jytte the wrong way, though, and she obviously does not like her. But we have a nice dinner, including some excellent fish soup, and head back to the albergue.

Jytte gets into the pool, while Tom and I sit on the side and dangle our feet in the cool water. We talk and watch a man and his two young sons play in the shallow end, as the sun sets and another fine day comes to a close.

June 28

Not a whole heckuva lot of other excitement to report today, folks, although I did have a delicious pizza for dinner tonight at an outdoor cafe in Sahagun. We slogged it through the hot and dry meseta for 24 kilometers or so today, and stopped by Moratinos for a visit with Rebekah, a former Pittsburgh resident and journalist who now lives in a tiny village in Spain on the Camino. I became acquainted with her on the Camino chat forum I discovered awhile back, and wanted to put a face with the name. It was a nice visit, and then we hit the trail again and eventually made it to Sahagun, where we checked into the municipal hostel and promptly ran into Alf and Anita, our friends from Norway.

More later...

It was a hot and dry walk into Sahagun, and we had to look around some for the municipal albergue. At one point, we walked past a group of senors sitting outside a bar and they pointed us farther down the road. Eventually, we find the place in the middle of downtown. It's a cool facility, though, located in a big, converted church, with the large dormitory upstairs. The ceilings are high, and the bunks are separated into roomy, four-bed cubicles, so it is pretty comfortable. Lots of people are here, but the high ceilings seem to cut down on the noise and it's nice and quiet.

After a nice shower, I wash clothes in a bathroom sink and there is a clothesline stretched along the wall in our cubicle, so I hang my wet laundry there. Tom is in the bed across from me, and Anita and Alf are in the other two bunks. Jytte takes a bunk nearby, in the cubicle across the aisle.

June 29

*W*e are still in Sahagun this morning (Wednesday), waiting to board a train to Ponferrada. From there, we'll bus to Sarria, and rejoin the Camino. I pretty greatly overestimated myself and underestimated the difficulty of the walking, and consequently am running out of time to walk the entire Frances route before I have to be back in Madrid for my flight home. So I'm jumping ahead to save some days. And my friends, Tom and Jytte, are coming with me, so we can share the experience of walking together into Santiago de Compostela. The three of us have become good friends over the past two weeks. They are wonderful people, and I am honored that they want to share the end of our journey with me. I think we will be friends for life.

So we should be there in about a week, in Santiago. If we arrive early, we may go on to Finisterre, a spot on the Atlantic Ocean that once was known as the end of the world. Some people say it's not a real Camino unless you walk the entire distance. A bunch of rot, I say. To me, it doesn't matter. This whole thing has been an incredible experience, and having to skip ahead by train and/or bus doesn't take anything away.

So we'll be in Sarria sometime this evening, and start walking again in the morning. See you then ...

This is where we said goodbye to Alf and Anita. They are running out of vacation time and will be heading back home to Norway after they arrive in Leon, another two days of walking. We all stayed together in the municipal albergue in downtown Sahagun, and had a great dinner at an outdoor café. Lots of lively conversation and laughing. Alf is hilarious, with a dry sense of humor and plenty of wisecracks about Sweden. Apparently, the Swedes are the butt of jokes in Norway much the same way as the A&M Aggies are the butt of jokes here in Texas. Pretty funny.

The city's big albergue here is pretty cool. It is located inside a huge, converted church building, with high, heavy beam raftered ceilings, and the floor plan is nice and roomy. There are 64 bunk beds upstairs in cubicles of eight beds each, and there is plenty of space to maneuver and walk around. I think the high ceilings help with the noise level, too, so it's a fairly relaxing place.

With only a few exceptions, everywhere we've stayed has been fairly comfortable. Clean, comfortable beds, decent pillows, clean blankets available. Never ran into any problems with bedbugs or anything like that. Clean bathrooms. Warm showers. Aside from the first few days, I always slept pretty well, and sleeping is a big issue for me. Walking all day long and drinking a little alcohol before bedtime probably helped, but I'd just put in my earplugs and usually get a decent night's sleep.

We normally went to bed around 9 or 10, and almost always woke up by 6 a.m. – earlier if there were stomping feet and roving flashlight beams from fellow pilgrims. I'm not a big fan of getting out of bed early in the morning, but this was different and I didn't really mind it, although I definitely enjoyed the times we stayed in private rooms and slept an hour or two later than normal.

June 29 (later the same day)

I '*m sitting in a beautiful, tree-filled park in downtown Ponferrada, after a nearly 3-hour train ride from Sahagun. We've crossed over the seemingly endless meseta and into the mountainous Galicia region. This was my first train ride and it was pretty cool. I may have to try a little train trip when I get back home.*

In about an hour, we'll catch a bus to Sarria, where we'll spend the night and head out in the morning. It should take 5-6 days' walking to reach Santiago.

I'm feeling kinda tired today, and it was strange to sit and watch the countryside go by, instead of being out walking in it. What we covered in a few hours would have taken 8 or 9 days on foot.

So far, it looks like I've walked 351.7 kilometers since I started in Pamplona on June 11, but who's counting? That's about 211 miles, a little over 11 miles a day. No, wait. We didn't walk at all today, and only did 6 kilometers a few days ago, so let's bump that up to 12 miles a day. Doesn't seem like much, considering I was walking 12 miles in 3 hours, 40 minutes at home, getting ready for this. I figured I could do at least 18-20 miles a day here, and finish in 24 to 26 days. Ha!

The very first day was 17.4 kilometers, a little over 10 miles, and it kicked my dadgum arse. I was wiped out. Then the famous blister erupted, but even if that hadn't happened, I still don't think I could have done much more than 15-16 miles a day. The terrain is just too tough. It ain't like walking down alongside the highway in Texas. The path goes up, up, up, down, down, down, this way, that way, over, under, around ... and even after your legs finally start getting conditioned to it, your feet continue to take a pounding. I don't know. Maybe I'm just old. We had dinner one evening with a young Australian kid who said he was doing 47 kilometers a day. Good grief ...

So, if there is a next time, and I have a feeling there will be eventually, I will allow a full six weeks to cover the distance. This time, I only allowed a little over 4 weeks. Not nearly enough time.

Nevertheless, it's been an amazing time, and I have no regrets. I'd liked to have walked the whole way, but it's OK. I've challenged myself in a big way and succeeded, broken through a huge wall of fear and anxiety, shown quite a bit of courage, realized things that are important to me, began to understand what it means to love myself and that I'm not such a bad guy despite my many faults, met some wonderful people and made at least two new lifelong friends ... and found out that my beliefs about spirituality and such are not so crazy or uncommon after all. Oh, and that there are a heckuva lot of nice people out there in the world ...

June 30

*I*t couldn't have been much better.
After yesterday's energy-draining day of train and bus rides, today was close to perfection. I'm not sure it could have been any better: clear, blue skies; temperature around 70 degrees; cool breeze in the air...

Such a change from the day before, when we sat looking out windows of the train at the landscape whizzing by. It was a strange sensation, not being out there walking. We found ourselves searching, searching for signs of the Camino — a yellow arrow, a sign, something, anything. We missed it. The Camino.

Then came today. Back on the path, and all is well with the world. Possibly the best walking day so far. Through dense forests, along clear, cool streams. Past old stone houses and farms, with dogs resting in the sun, old men out for a walk. An easy and beautiful walking day. And a thinking day.

For some reason, I thought about my parents and my childhood, and the things that happened in my life that affected the kind of person I turned out to be. The decisions I made. The things that shaped my personality. Where do my raging insecurities come from, for example?

Sometimes, you think a lot when you walk.

Anyway ... this place we stopped for the day is completely beautiful and peaceful, at a little place called Mercadoiro, about 17.5 kilometers from Sarria. It's an incredible converted monastery. The entrance off the Camino is surrounded by tall stone walls that surround a garden and patio full of flowers, with tall trees shading everything. In the yard are big, blooming fruit trees: cherry, apple, fig. I picked a couple of cherries – delicious. A large, grassy lawn slopes away, then drops down to a view of an adjacent mountain, lush and green. I could live here ...

Tom and I crossing a long footbridge on the way out of Portomarin

This place, Mercadoiro, is fantastic. It actually is kind of hidden, and you don't know it's there until you're right on top of it. In many places walking through the woods, the Camino path is sort of sunken. How can I describe it ... the earth on either side of you as you walk is waist-high, shoulder-high, or higher, with thick woods and tall trees all around. To me, it seems like this could be the result of millions and millions of footsteps over the decades, wearing down the soil. Sometimes crude stone walls have been built, or wooden fences stretched to mark adjacent fields.

Suddenly, just up ahead there is a hand-written sign alongside the path. It is a menu, describing different types of food. The sign is next to a break in a tall stone wall, and there is soft music coming from inside. I step through the opening and see a large patio with a half-dozen tables and chairs, surrounded by a flowering garden, then a couple of beautiful old wood and stone buildings left and right, and a huge, sweeping lawn reaching out toward the mountains in the distance.

We'll stay here.

Tom and Jytte and I find beds in a room in the back corner of the dormitory. It's a large room with three sets of bunks, and a big window that later opens to the setting sun, and we have it all to ourselves. There are other rooms adjacent to this one, with other pilgrims staying there, but otherwise we're all alone.

We unpack and take turns using the bathroom and shower down the hall. Washing clothes in the sink outside and hanging them on the line to dry is next. What a place. It is owned by two brothers, and there is a newspaper clipping framed and hung on the wall next to the bar that talks about them renovating and opening the place. Apparently, they're doing pretty well with it, as Tom and I see them drive away that evening in a new Mercedes.

As I wrote in my journal, today was a grand day. Blue skies, temperature around 70 degrees at noon. When I stopped at a little bar to rest my feet and change socks, I had to put on my fleece pullover and sit in the sun to stay warm. It's probably 100 degrees in Texas today!

It was also a pretty serious thinking day. Over the last 10 kilometers or so, I was walking by myself, and I thought a lot about my parents and my childhood, and the things that happened in my life that affected the kind of person I turned out to be. The decisions I made. The events that shaped my personality. Where do my raging insecurities come from? My self-esteem issues?

About the insecurities, a counselor I spoke to several years ago suggested that I may have been an unwanted child. Babies who are unwanted, she said, pick up these feelings in the womb, and carry them throughout their lives. I don't know. Maybe that was it. Maybe I never really felt safe around my parents. Never really trusted them. Ours was not a warm, loving home. My parents took care of me physically, yes, but my father definitely hurt me with words and with lack of words, lack of attention, lack of affection, and my mother hurt me with some pretty severe spankings. She is dead now, and so I cannot ask her about these things, but I'm pretty sure my mother wanted me and always loved me. My father, on the other hand, I was never really sure about. His love seemed to be mostly conditional. And I never felt like I met those conditions. I never lived up to his expectations, and never really felt that he was proud of me, or really loved me.

I know my relationship with my father affected me a lot. The first time I remember him ever hugging me was when I was 26 years old. It felt really uncomfortable, and I did not hug him back. This was a few years after my parents were divorced.

My father was not much of a communicator. Our family never talked about anything meaningful, really, that I can remember. No lively conversations around the dinner table. No going to mom and dad to discuss childhood problems. No reassuring embraces, and "It'll be OK." I'll never forget my younger sister telling me one time that she remembers going to my father to talk about some issue she was having, and that she was feeling hurt or angry or whatever. His response was this: "Well, don't feel that way." Oh, OK, thanks, dad.

Pretty much the extent of my relationship with my dad when I was a kid centered around sports. I started playing Little League baseball and peewee football when I was eight years old, and it didn't take long before I was pretty good at both. I played tailback and defensive end when our football team won the league championship. And I pitched two no-hitters when I was 12 and was the no. 1 pitcher on the all-star team.

Unfortunately, that was pretty much the extent of my athletic career. I played two more years of baseball and football after that, and started running track and playing basketball at school when I entered seventh grade. I made the all-star team both of those years in baseball and won lots of medals and ribbons and stuff in track. Our basketball team wasn't much to talk about, but I started at guard in junior high because I had a really good little jump shot and could handle the ball.

When I was in 10th grade, I quit playing sports altogether. Now, sports had been my life since I was eight years old. I loved sports. I lived and breathed sports. But, one by one, I quit them all. It was a combination of reasons: nagging injuries that year (broken big toe, pulled hamstring, Achilles tendon), burn-out and bad attitude. The attitude problem had been growing for a couple of years. It started the day after I pitched that all-star baseball game when I was 12.

Making the all-star team and getting the nod as the team's starting pitcher was the highlight of my life to that point. It was my first year to make all-stars, and I was the starting pitcher! And this was no lightweight team, folks. There were some great little athletes at the Oaks Dads Club, in northwest Houston. Our shortstop went on to star on his high school football and basketball teams, making all-state in both sports, and is in the Hall of Fame at his university after quarterbacking their football team to a small college national championship.

So, for me, this was the ultimate. I had worked really hard on my pitching, and here I was, the top pitcher in the league. So the day of our first game comes, and we go up against the other all-star team from Oaks Dads. They had two 10-12 year old leagues there, the National league and the American league. I was in the National league. The winner of this game advances in the tournament that eventually leads to the Little League World Series.

There is a huge crowd at the game. People sitting and standing everywhere. The lights are bright and the cheering loud and raucous. We are home team, so I take the mound to start the first inning. I'm a little nervous, but not too bad. They've got some really good hitters over there, but I never really got nervous pitching. The first pitch, I sent a fastball, low and right down the middle, and their leadoff hitter smacked it on the ground to shortstop. Easy out. Unfortunately, our shortstop didn't get his glove all the way down, and the ball skidded out to left field. Runner on first.

Next batter, same thing. I sent the first pitch low, right over the middle, he slapped it on the ground to shortstop, and the ball skidded underneath his glove and out into left field. Runners at first and second, no outs.

Shit. Now I'm freaking out a little bit. Both of those should have been easy outs. Two pitches, two men on base, and their best hitters are coming up.

Our catcher signals for another fastball, and I shake him off. A sharp-breaking curve is my strikeout pitch, and I'm not about to let this next guy hit the damn ball. Nobody can hit my curve, and I can pretty much throw it wherever I want: over the plate and breaking outside; inside and breaking down over the plate. One of my favorite pitches was to fire a curve right at the batter's shoulder. At the last second, the ball would break down and across into the catcher's mitt, as the batter was usually picking himself up out of the dirt after bailing out.

Anyway, I struck the next three batters out with curveballs, and continued throwing nothing but curveballs the rest of the game. Our catcher kept calling for fastballs, and I kept shaking him off. We took something like a 4-0 lead into the fourth inning, I think it was, and that's when my arm gave out. Snapping off curveballs is hard on the elbow, and I had thrown a bunch of them. Also, the other team had started to pick up on the fact that I was throwing nothing but curves. I heard their third-base coach screaming, "It's all curves; it's all curves!" But I kept throwing the breaking stuff. I just couldn't make myself throw another fastball.

And I started walking people. My arm got tired from all the strain, and I couldn't put my pitches where I wanted them. And the other team stopped swinging at pitches that curved outside the strike zone. I walked four guys in a row, and our coach pulled me out of the game, with the bases loaded and no outs. We got out of that inning with a 4-2 lead intact, but I watched from the bench in disbelief as the American League rallied in the bottom of the sixth to win the game 5-4.

Now, this is the important part of this whole story. I was not the losing pitcher, because we still had the lead at the end of the inning after I was pulled. The loss officially went to another one of our pitchers. So I was naturally upset, tears and all, about us losing the game, but at least I was not the losing pitcher. That would have been completely devastating. It wouldn't have mattered what anyone said to me. It would have been completely my fault that we lost. That's just the way I would have looked at it.

We lost the game and that really sucked, but I took some consolation in knowing that it was not my fault we lost. It was one of our other pitchers who gave up the winning runs.

Until the next day.

I was laying on the couch at home watching cartoons on television, and my dad was standing in the hall doorway. We were talking about last night's game. I don't remember what all was said, but I'll never forget him saying: "Well, if our top pitcher hadn't been throwing curveballs all night, we probably would have won the game." Apparently, somebody sitting in the stands behind home plate had told my dad after the game that every pitch I threw after those first two fastballs was a curve.

To say I was devastated is an understatement. I was completely floored. I've always said it felt like I'd been run over by a Mack truck. He was saying that I was the reason we lost the game. Maybe that's not what he meant, but that's sure what I heard.

The biggest achievement of my life had just been flattened by a steamroller. And my dad was the one driving the steamroller. I can look back and see that moment as the beginning of the decline of our relationship. Up to that point, my dad was pretty much my hero. He was a big guy who could do just about anything, it seemed. He could fix cars and build all kinds of stuff. I worked my ass off to try and make him proud of me, and now he had crushed me. Just crushed me.

I played sports for another two years after that and enjoyed quite a bit of success, then just chucked it all during my sophomore year. And when I did that, I also chucked my identity. Without sports, I had no idea who I was any more. I always measured my self-worth by my accomplishments on the field, the court, the track. Without any of that, I was nothing. I was pretty much lost for quite awhile after that, and I still have regrets to this day.

But that was a long time ago, and I've come to realize that my father did the best he could – both my parents did the best they could. And I don't blame them for anything, anymore. Well, not much, anyway. Parents are just people. They make mistakes. They are not perfect. I'm a parent, and I've made a lot of mistakes. Mistakes that have hurt both my daughters. And I love them deeply. I would never want to hurt either one of them, but I know I have.

Heavy stuff, eh? Well, that's the kind of day it was – a day for thinking.

Another thing I think that affected me growing up was the Vietnam war. I was born in 1957, and I can remember watching a lot of television news coverage of the war as a kid. And for some weird reason – remember, my family did not talk about much of anything – my reaction to seeing all of this stuff on TV was this: "When I turn 18, I'm gonna start smoking cigarettes, because I'm gonna get drafted, go to Vietnam and die, anyway.

Bizarre, eh? But I can remember thinking that, as I was growing up. I never told anybody else, but I just thought that when I turned 18, I was going to be drafted into the Army, go to Vietnam, and die. That was my destiny. I really thought that. That must have had some kind of effect on a kid …

July 1

He walked out of his barn and headed in my direction. If a movie casting director were looking for someone to fill the role of an old Spanish farmer, this guy would be perfect. As he got closer, I said, "Buenos dias." He returned my greeting, and then said something I didn't quite understand. My mental translator doesn't work as quickly as the words come. So I asked him to repeat: "¿Como?" He said it again and this time I got it. He was telling me it was a fine day for walking. I smiled and extended my hand and he shook it, and he smiled and said, "Buen Camino." I said, "Gracias," and was on my way again. Awesome.

And so it was ... a fine day for walking. At least until the afternoon, when the path took us out of the forests and the protection of the shade, and away from the villages and farms. It got hot and a lot of the walking was across and alongside asphalt roadways.

We stopped at some godforsaken place called Gonzar to rest, then headed on to Ligonde, where we spent the night. Had a good rest and then walked nearly all day today to reach Melide. We're a few days away from Santiago now, and I'm having to fight my monkey brain and crazy thoughts, which are trying to spoil the end of the journey by speeding ahead to the end and wanting it all to be over and me back at home.

So I think the big lesson for me this last week of the trip is to learn to enjoy the moment and the day. To live one day at a time. I always live either in the past or in the future, regretting the past and worrying about the future. Neither one of those things has a whole heckuva lot to do with reality ...

I took a little rest stop and fell behind Tom and Jytte for awhile, then caught up with them at a bar outside a place called Gonzar. They were glad to see me, and that made me feel pretty good. Both of them were a little shaken, and said they had walked down into the town, wondering if I had gone that way, and felt a really creepy vibe as they walked around. Lots of dogs tied up, skinny, bad coats, obviously not being taken care of properly. Jytte is one of these intuitive, highly sensitive people who easily absorbs negative energy. She was really freaked out by it all.

This is my second stop in the shade in the last hour-and-a-half. A beautiful morning has turned into a slog, and my mind has also gone into some serious negative thinking. I can't quite put my finger on it.

I've always found it incredibly difficult, even impossible, to identify my emotions. I can't say, well, I'm feeling this, or I'm feeling that. I either feel bad, or I feel good. Don't ask me why. I probably don't know why. But I do know that I'm thinking way too much right now about home, and not thinking enough about the here and now. About today. Right now. I always focus on the negative. Dwell on it, mash it, twist it, turn it over and over, slice it, dice it ... and is any of it real? Most likely, not much. Maybe not at all. But can I let it go? Maybe set it aside, and think about it later? My mother always told me, "Son, don't borrow trouble." I never really understood that. I do now, but just because I understand it doesn't mean that I don't borrow trouble. I do it all the time.

Anyway, we sit outside the bar for awhile, have a couple cervezas and a nice boccadillo. We have about an hour's walking left, I think, before we reach our destination for the day at Ligonde, a small village with what looks to be a nice little albergue.

I got pretty far ahead of Tom and Jytte after we left Gonzar, and thought for awhile that I'd lost them completely. Ligonde is a tiny, little place and I took a wrong turn at one point, about halfway through town. A bunch of people were sitting in chairs outside someone's house, and as I passed by them, they called out (in Spanish), "Hey, pilgrim, this is the wrong way. Go the other way." I smiled and waved, thanked them and retraced my steps, and sure enough, soon found the albergue I was looking for. It was a pretty nice place, with 22 beds in a large, roomy dormitory, but there was no one there.

The front door was open, so I went inside, and I heard a shower running in the women's bathroom. I figured maybe it was the proprietor, so I took off my backpack and my shoes, and sat down on a set of steps just inside the front door. Pretty soon, a woman comes out of the bathroom and I try to ask her about staying there, but it was a severe communication breakdown. I think she understood what I was asking, but I definitely did not understand what she was answering.

Eventually, after lots of gesturing and pointing and such, I realized she was telling me that I needed to go just up the road to a restaurant you could see from the front steps, where I could register to spend the night at the albergue. She was just another pilgrim staying there, it turned out, and she gave me the name of the person I needed to see at the restaurant.

So I walk down there, around a big cow pasture with cattle grazing, and see three women sitting at one of the tables outside. I say hello, and ask for the hospitalera and she is one of the three. I arrange to spend the night back at the albergue, then go inside and order a tall San Miguel. It's a nice little bar and restaurant, and I'm sitting at a corner table when I see Tom walking up the path. I thought I had lost him, and was preparing to make the rest of the journey alone. But there he was! It was great to see him striding up the road. He joins me inside and we find out about dinner, then eventually make our way back to the albergue, where we shower and change, wash and hang up our clothes in the yard.

The albergue is very nice, with only a handful of people spending the night. We have the pilgrim's menu back at the restaurant, along with some wine and another cerveza or two, then head back to the albergue. It is cool and quiet, maybe eight people spending the night, and we have a good rest, before heading out the next day.

July 3

*G*oodness gracious, what a night. Another large municipal
albergue; another nightmare ...
*Imagine this, y'all: you walk into this big building after a long, hard
day of walking, register at the front desk and pay 5 euros, and they
assign you a bunk. Give you a little ticket with a bed number on it.
You walk upstairs and there's a big room full of bunk beds, squeezed
together so that there's enough room for one person at a time to walk
between the beds, and people everywhere. Some of the people are either
completely self-absorbed, just plain rude, or idiots. So, you find your
bunk and try to get ready to shower, sitting on your bed and digging
through your backpack, while people basically are climbing over you or
squeezing around you, doing the same thing. You find some clean
clothes, your towel and soap, then go back downstairs to the duchas,
where you strip down and take a shower, possibly with a dozen other
people. Finish the shower, get dressed, head back upstairs to the sardine
can to square things away at the bunk. Forget about washing clothes,
which is usually the second chore. This place is such a zoo that all you
want to do is get the hell out and head downtown somewhere for a cool
drink and dinner later.*

*At 10 p.m., it's lights out and time for bed, but people continue to
yak, yak, yak, in any number of different languages until all hours. At
1 a.m., you're still awake and just wanting the night to be over. By 5*

a.m., people are starting to get up and rummage around in their backpacks, flashlights whipping around the room, or lights glowing from bunks, shining in your eyes ...

That's pretty much how it goes in the big-city municipals. Avoid them at all costs. If you want pleasant evenings, plan your stops to avoid the more popular and crowded spots.

Aim for the places out in the country, like the place we stopped for lunch today. Another beautiful, out-of-the-way cafe, beautiful patio and garden, cool breeze. We've stayed there for a couple hours, just relaxing and getting ready to walk another few kilometers to another small village, where we will spend the night. Two or three more days to Santiago. Ciao, y'all ...

Ah, this was Melide, a really nice little town but a horrible albergue. Nothing wrong with the place, actually – clean, modern, well-run, nice facilities – but these large municipal albergues are just the pits. After a quiet, peaceful night in the country at Ligonde, and the paradise of Mercadoiro, this place is just the opposite. Too crowded. Too many people. Too hectic. Bad energy. When you compare this place to something like Ventosa or Villamayor del Rio or Atapuerca, there's just no comparison.

It was lights out at 10 p.m. at the Melide municipal, just like a lot of other places. However, that didn't mean people went to bed at 10 p.m. We were in a huge dormitory and the conversations in any number of different languages went on and on and on. Thank goodness for ear plugs.

Tom and I were in bottom bunks across from each other, and in the morning, the guy who was sleeping above him actually hung a flashlight on his bedpost at 5 a.m. and left it there, while he tromped back and forth to the bathroom a few times, and noisily packed his backpack.

People are people, and it's all part of the deal, I know, but like I said, stick to the smaller, more out-of-the-way albergues, and I think you'll have a much better experience.

After we check in and get showered and changed, we immediately head outside and down the street for a cold beverage and something to eat. It's a few blocks uptown to what appears to be the primary gathering spot – sort of a combination city park and restaurant and bar. It is beautiful. Heavily shaded by tall trees, with park benches all along the perimeter, tables and chairs scattered around. We sit and talk and people-watch, and drink a tall cerveza.

For dinner that night, we had hamburgers and french fries. They have delicious hamburgers over here. Twice I had a "hamberguesa completo," which comes with the usual lettuce, tomato, pickles, all that stuff, and to finish it off, a fried egg atop the meat. It's fantastic.

July 4

O *K, folks, after an almost rest-free night in Melide, all is again right with the world ...*

We headed out fairly early this morning, after a delicious and hit-the-spot cafe con leche and croissant with mermelada, and had a fairly easy 14-kilometer stroll through the countryside to Ribadiso, where we stopped for lunch and rest. It is a beautiful spot, with outdoor patio and flowery garden. I had a tasty bowl of lentil soup with chopped onion and locally made cheese. Then it was on to Arzua, billed as the last major population center (7,000 people) before Santiago, and home to a 14th century Augustinian church.

To facilitate our recovery from last night's ordeal, we checked into a nice little pension (hotel) on the main drag entering town. To share a room, it cost Tom and me an extra 10 euros each, compared to the price of the average albergue, and it is a slice of paradise. The only thing keeping it from being the whole paradise pie is the lack of a bathtub. There's a nice shower, but no tub, so consequently no bubble bath. The room is sort of small, but clean and cool. It's fantastic. I can hear Tom singing in the bathroom. He doesn't sing very often ...

So we'll chill here for awhile, then go out later for some calamari and some pulpo (octopus). Yes, octopus. It's a speciality here. I had some back in Logrono, and it's pretty good stuff, y'all. They boil the thing for awhile, then cut it up into chunks and flavor it with olive oil and sweet paprika. It´s got kind of a firm, chewy-but-not-too-chewy texture and tastes really good. I´d find a recipe and maybe have an octopus cookout when I get home, but I don´t think they have any pulpo at HEB ...

Self-portrait in front of a marker indicating 60 kilometers to Santiago

I guess this is a good place to talk about food on the Camino. We usually had a café con leche (espresso with steamed milk) and a croissant or toast for breakfast. Sometimes first thing in the morning; sometimes we'd walk for awhile and then stop at a bar or restaurant somewhere. It usually cost between two and three euros for breakfast.

The places we stopped ranged from a hole-in-the-wall with plastic tables and chairs outside, to really nice cafes and restaurants. More often than not, you drop your backpack outside, then go in and order whatever from the bar, wait a minute or two and then take your stuff back outside. Sometimes you paid when you got your food and drink, but a lot of times they didn't want your money until you were finished. I wondered how often people take off without paying.

Lunch usually came during our midday break, and what is very common is a boccadillo, or sandwich. Sometimes these are pretty good; sometimes not so great. I had some fantastic tortilla y patata boccadillos, with several slices of warm egg and potato omelet inside a soft roll of bread. Then one time, I ordered a chorizo (sausage) boccadillo, and it came on a very dry, hard roll, with a half-dozen or so small, round slices of sausage. That's it. I asked Tom about this dry, hard bread that they served with almost everything, and he said it is basically a mixture of flour and water, designed to be cheap and filling.

For dinner, sometimes we had the local pilgrim's menu, which includes three courses for prices ranging from seven to 10 euros, depending on the place. The menu might include salad, entrée and dessert, for example, and a bottle of red wine. At one place, they gave us two bottles of wine with our meal. Wine is a big deal in Spain, and it is here I guess I can explain that my imbibing on the Camino broke a 22-year stretch of being a teetotaler for me. I describe in my book, "Finding God in Texas," how a simple, desperate prayer in May 1989 rescued me from a pretty severe drinking problem that cost me a marriage and several jobs. I was basically drunk every day at that point in my life, and had been that way for a number of years.

I was broke, divorced, alone and closer than I knew at the time to living under a bridge, and now I am a homeowner with a fine career and enough money to enjoy life and even travel overseas. So why in the world would I go back to drinking?

Well, as I researched my Camino trip, I came across something that talked about the importance of wine with meals in Spain. There was some saying in Spanish that I haven't been able to find again that basically said a meal without wine is not a meal. As I was to be fully immersed in that culture for at least a month, I thought maybe I should experience this part of it, too.

And I thought about what a holistic healer had told me during a two-day workshop I attended several years ago on detoxing the body, natural healing and healthy eating. A major part of the process during this workshop included drinking a gallon of a special tea mixture designed to remove toxins from the liver, and I ask this guy if my habit of smoking cigars would undo the benefits of this cleansing.

He said, no, not necessarily. I wish I could explain it as well as he did, but basically he said that it depends on the reasons a person smokes, whether it will be harmful to them. If a person is high-strung, stressed-out, nervous, tense, puffing away, puffing away, then the smoking will likely be harmful. However, if one is calm and peaceful, simply enjoying the tobacco, grateful for the tobacco, then there is likely to be no harm.

With alcohol, in the old days, I drank to get intoxicated. Plain and simple. I liked to get drunk, and that's why I drank. Always. It was never for the enjoyment of the beer, wine, whiskey or whatever I was drinking. The whole idea was to change the way I felt. To get loaded. Escape from reality. Which is not a good reason, and that's why it caused me such problems. If I were drinking to enjoy the wine, to complement the meal, and not to get drunk, that is a good reason. That is the purpose of the wine. I thought a lot about it, and I asked a couple of people what they thought. And I finally decided that if it felt right, I would do it. And I did.

I had two cans of San Miguel when I arrived in Pamplona, and I had white wine with my paella. Guess what? I didn't get drunk, and I didn't want to get drunk. It was OK, and I came to the honest conclusion that I do not have a so-called disease that makes it impossible for me to drink normally. To have a couple of drinks and no more. There is not a monster inside of me waiting to destroy me if I feed it alcohol. I just don't believe that any more. But that's just me. Other people are free to believe what they want about addiction being an incurable disease. I don't have a problem with that. I just don't agree with it any more, for me.

And the beer in Spain was very good, as was the wine. At the end of a long day of hiking, an ice-cold San Miguel draft was wonderful. Tom even introduced me to cognac, which is a delicious after-dinner drink. It is almost better to swirl and smell the aroma from a glass of cognac than it is to drink it. Warm and delicious and smooth as it goes down.

The weather in northern Spain is also fantastic. It is one of the primary reasons Tom decided to retire there, on the Atlantic coast. While I was there, in June and early July, it was in the 60s and 70s, most of the time. They had a little heat wave for several days, and it got a little warmer for awhile, but a lot of times, I wore my fleece pullover for several hours in the morning to stay warm.

My wardrobe included two moisture-wicking T-shirts from an army surplus store, an old collared moisture-wicking golf shirt, two pair of lightweight cargo shorts, three pair of boxer shorts, several pair of hiking socks, and a floppy hat to shade the sun. The shorts had lots of pockets, and I stuffed all kinds of things in there. I wore a "neck safe" around my neck, under my shirt, to carry my passport, ATM card, credit card, and pilgrim's credentials. The only time the neck safe ever left my neck was when I took a shower, and even then it was never out of my sight.

The pilgrim's credential is a fold-up card that you get stamped every night at the albergue where you stay. You can also get it stamped at various bars and other places along the way. The purpose is to prove that you are walking the Camino, and it is required to stay in the albergues. I got mine by mail from the American Pilgrims on the Camino organization in Palo Alto, California.

July 5

S logging through the rain today and nearing the outskirts of Santiago de Compostela. Heck, I think I am already in the outskirts, but I have no idea where I am, really, just following the Camino.

It's kind of a bittersweet day, 'cause this is the finale, everything I've been limping and hurting and panting and sweating toward for the past four weeks. And I'm also looking forward to going home. I've never been away from home for this long, folks, never. So there's a lot of mixed feelings today.

More later, gotta go ...

Yesterday was July 4, a national holiday back in the United States — Independence Day — but just another day over here. In America, of course, it's a day off from work and a time for backyard barbecues, picnics at the lake, and fireworks. In Spain, just another mid-summer day. Felt a little strange.

As we got closer and closer to Santiago and the end of the road, I began to have a lot of mixed emotions. I did not want it to be over. After such a traumatic start back in Madrid, I've gotten very comfortable walking the Camino, living this simple life, spending my days and nights with these fantastic people, and I don't want to say goodbye.

Skies are overcast and it starts misting rain early this morning, and this is the first time I've had to break out the poncho I've been carrying strapped to my backpack. Tom swears up and down it is not raining. It is nothing more than a low cloud, he says, although the water dripping off the brim of my hat feels like rain to me.

We head up the road about a half-mile to where Jytte is staying, at the municipal albergue in Santa Irene. Tom and I spent the night at a private albergue, after we lost track of Jytte back in Arzua. We all spent the night there at the same hotel, a nice little place above a restaurant, with Tom and I sharing a room, and Jytte just down the hall. We had a wonderful time that night, with pulpo for dinner, a nice bottle of wine, and a couple of glasses of cognac for dessert.

As we sat at a sidewalk table outside a crowded bar near our hotel, Jytte got a little tipsy from the cognac and could not stop giggling at something that was said. That got Tom and me laughing, too, and we ordered another round, and laughed and talked until sunset, and it was time to get back upstairs to bed.

In the morning, Tom was already up and dressed and gone before I rolled out of bed. No big deal. He was either waiting somewhere outside, or he had taken off already and I would catch up to him at some point.

So I brushed my teeth and washed my face, put in my contact lens, got dressed, squared my backpack away and headed downstairs. Tom was sitting outside the restaurant next door, drinking a cup of coffee, and he was ready to get started. I went inside and got some coffee, and while I sat and drank it, Tom headed back upstairs to find Jytte, who was nowhere to be seen. He came back and said he knocked on her door and got no response, so she must have gotten up early and hit the road. It was around eight o'clock by then, and there was no way she was still in bed. Jytte had sleeping issues, and she was usually the first one out of bed. We figured she must have gotten tired of waiting for us this morning, since we'd decided to sleep in a little bit. As Jytte was so fond of saying, "No problem!" We will run into her up ahead at some point today.

So, properly fueled by the delicious café con leche and a fresh croissant, off we go. Unfortunately, we never did find Jytte. We decided to stop for the night in Santa Irene, just outside Arca de Pino, which is the beginning of the last stage of walking before you reach Santiago. Remember, the most comfortable places we stayed were always in-between the official stages listed in Camino guidebooks. There were two albergues listed for Santa Irene, a municipal and a private. We opted for the private, which was more expensive than the municipal — 10 euros compared to five — but also likely to be less crowded.

Indeed it was.

When you step inside, you are in the dining room, with a large sitting area off to the right, complete with a couch and chair, coffee table, books and magazines, television set. Left of the dining room is a large kitchen. Bathrooms are down the hall, with individual showers on one side, sinks and toilets on the other side. Beyond that is a beautiful, small dormitory, dark and cool and quiet, with a total of 15 very comfortable beds on two levels, leading to a huge backyard and flower garden. After checking in and cleaning up, washing clothes, we sit outside at a picnic table, beneath a ceiling of thick grapevines, heavy with clumps of green grapes, me sipping a cold beer and Tom a glass of dry, white wine.

Later, we had a communal dinner with what turned out to be a bunch of school teachers. Three of them — two young ladies and a young man, probably in their late 30s to early 40s – were from Denmark, while an older, married couple were from the U.S., somewhere up north, but living and teaching school on an American military base in Germany. They were traveling the Camino on rented bicycles and talked about having all kinds of mechanical problems with the bikes.

By the way, we did eventually find Jytte, who it turned out was staying in the municipal albergue a few hundred meters up the road. Apparently, when Tom went back inside the hotel this morning in Arzua to find her, he knocked on the wrong door. He knocked on room 4 and she was in room 5, or vice versa. Nevertheless, Jytte was quite upset by it all, thinking we had purposely left her behind. She never said as much, but it was pretty obvious. When we discovered where she was, we walked down there and found her, and did our best to explain what had really happened, but I'm not sure she really believed our story. Nevertheless, we agreed to meet the next morning and head for Santiago.

July 6

*W*ell, folks, made it to Santiago yesterday and attended the pilgrim's mass at noon today. Kinda cool to witness it in person, but basically one of those mind-numbing church services. Sorry, but it is. The cathedral is an amazing place and the old town area is really cool. No burning bush experiences to report, just a satisfying end to a really cool and amazing experience. There will probably be more to report after it all sinks in and settles for awhile.

It's been quite a trip, and I'm ready to get home.

We had a nice send-off dinner last night with Tom, Jytte, me, Enzo and Maria, a wonderful couple from Italy with whom we've spent quite a bit of time in the last week or so. Warm, excellent people -- "Do ya know what ah mean-a?"

Ciao, y'all ...

Tom, a Norwegian living in Spain, and Enzo, an
Italian from Sicily, talk about life and happiness over a
glass of brandy

Group selfie with friends on the way to Santiago

Pilgrims gathering outside the cathedral in Santiago de Compostela

Tom, Jytte and I were supposed to walk into Santiago de Compostela together today, sharing the experience of completing our journey. Unfortunately, things did not quite turn out as planned.

We stopped for breakfast at a neighborhood bar in Arca de Pino, a little soaked from three kilometers of walking in the "low cloud" that Tom insisted was not rain. Some guy was sitting at the bar drinking whiskey at 8 o'clock in the morning, but we had coffee and even though the place really didn't serve much in the way of food, the proprietor graciously agreed to make us some toast. It was good toast, too. Thick slices of bread, sort of like good ol' Texas toast.

Then we geared up and headed back out into the low cloud, onward to Santiago. It was drizzling on and off, and at one point, Jytte and I were walking together through a wooded area, with Tom trailing a ways behind, and we were talking about this and that, when I asked her why she had decided to change her plans and walk with me to Santiago.

This was Jytte's second Camino, and this time she had started her journey with a female friend. The friend, whose name I can't remember, apparently bit off more than she could chew, however, and did not enjoy the walking. Did not enjoy it at all. Jytte told me shortly after we met back in Lorca that her friend was constantly complaining, and it wasn't long after that she called it quits and went back home to Denmark.

Anyway, Jytte and I had had some excellent discussions about a lot of things, including ego, and she helped me understand for the first time what ego is all about, and the problems it can cause – the problems it so often causes. I've done some reading since then, and understand it a little bit more. It turns out, friends, that ego is usually the source of so many problems. Ego causes hurt feelings, jealousy, resentment, envy, greed, all those kinds of things.

It seems Jytte's friend bailing out on her was upsetting, and threw a big wrench into her plans. To make a long story a little shorter, Jytte had contacted another friend back in Denmark, who was scheduled to come and join her in a week or so in Sarria, then they would make the walk together into Santiago.

She was not under the same time constraints that I was, and Jytte is pretty much at home wherever she is at the moment, so when I asked her one morning if she had any interest in jumping ahead with me and sharing the walk into Santiago de Compostela, she said, "Yes, I would like that."

I had asked Tom a few days before if he would consider joining me when I skipped ahead, and he said, no. "If I get on a train, it will be to go home," he said. It had been a rough journey for Tom, with a lot of physical pain, but he was determined to walk the entire route.

After Jytte decided to come with me, though, I asked Tom again. We were sitting in the yard of some restaurant/albergue, drinking our morning coffee, and I told him that it would be grand if the three of us walked into Santiago together, and would he reconsider. He said he would think about it. Later in the day, agreed to come with us.

Somehow, though, on that last day, something happened, something was said, and my feelings got hurt and Jytte's feeling got hurt, and she dropped back and I took off by myself. Ego got involved. Walking faster and faster, harder and harder. My legs were good and strong by this point, and I was really moving. I walked into Santiago by myself, and promptly ran smack into Enzo, in a large crowd of people milling around behind the magnificent cathedral. We hugged, and then there was Maria, more hugs and kissing of cheeks, and then Enzo took me to the pilgrim's office where they issue the Compostela certificate, a document written in Latin that verifies you are an official pilgrim who has successfully completed the Camino.

I ran into Tom and Jytte a little while later, and nothing was said about what had happened earlier. The five of us had dinner together that night, where we ate crepes and drank Sangria and champagne. Everyone took turns toasting the rest of the group, and when it was my turn to speak, I nearly couldn't get the words out. Tears choked my voice as I thanked them all for their friendship and love, and for showing me that I am worthy of being loved.

The next day, Maria and Enzo took off early for Finisterrae. Tom and Jytte and I met for breakfast at 10 a.m., then Jytte took off walking, also for Finisterrae. We stood and watched her go, waving as she turned around again and again, until she was out of sight. Tom was headed home to Coruna, and I was off to Madrid, to catch my flight home. First, we hung around and went together to the cathedral for the noon pilgrim's mass, then after retrieving our backpacks from a storeroom inside the pilgrim's office, we went our separate ways.

"I guess this is it," I said, as we stood on an old cobblestone street.

"This is it," Tom said.

I took a step forward and we hugged – kind of an awkward man hug with backpacks getting in the way – and that was it.

July 7

*W*as it real or just a dream?

Finishing the Camino was a pretty big let-down, and had me wondering whether it really was that special, or did I just make it all up? Did I just somehow fool myself into thinking that I was having such a great time? I´m supposed to be having this awesome experience, so I must be having an awesome experience, you know?

Or as my new Sicilian friend, Enzo, says, "Ya know what ah mean-a?"

Then today, I read some comments from other people on this great on-line Camino forum, about post-Camino blues. And once again, I learn ... I´m not unique. Damn! I´ve spent most of my life thinking I was pretty unique.

So, yeah, the Camino is indeed a special place, and leaving it can be sad. And I did, in fact, have a wonderful time, and shared a lot of that time with some wonderful people. And having to part company with those people is sad, too. We shared some pretty intense times out there.

But I will see them again, one of these days. Because even though I hate flying, I will come back. Maybe not to the Camino right away, but I will come back to Europe, I think, to see Tom, Enzo and Maria, Alf and Anita, Jytte, Paula ... all of these are tremendous people who showed me love and encouragement, and made me feel good about myself.

Hell, they liked me more than I like me! They accepted me for who I am, and chose to spend time with me. There was no kind of pretending going on – it's kinda hard to be anything other than yourself when you're showering, sleeping and going to the bathroom in the same room(s) with everyone else.

Our last night together, we had dinner at this really nice restaurant near the cathedral in Santiago. We had crepes. As we all took turns making farewell toasts, Maria – an Italian from Naples, who speaks no English at all – said in her toast (translated by Enzo) that I am a "good and interesting man." I asked Enzo later as we sat outside in the plaza having a nightcap to ask Maria what makes her think I am a good man. She only knew me for a week, for Pedro's sake. She said, it is in my face. I have a good and honest face, she said, touching her hand to it. That makes me want to cry, just thinking about it again.

So, it's normal to have post-Camino blues. Normal. That's good, and OK. And, yes, it was and is a special place, and an amazing experience that I will think about and write about for a long time. Oh, and one thing I've definitely figured out is the meaning of life, and the secret to happiness. It's really simple.

Love. That's all there is ...

So, even though I was scared spitless and wanted to come home almost as soon as I got there, traveling to Spain and walking the Camino was one of the best experiences of my life. It was truly life-changing. As a matter of fact, I returned two summers later, and walked it again, with Tom.

Tom is like an older version of me. We are similar in so many ways, although he is quite a bit wiser. We first met in June 2011, and have spent a total of around two months together, but we call each other "old friend." After walking the Camino a second time, including a climb over the Pyrenees mountains on the border with France, he invited me to spend a few days with him at his home in Coruna. It was fantastic. Here's an example of the kind of friend and person Tom is:

During Camino II, he and I both got a bad case of food poisoning one day. We managed to walk a few miles that morning, but we stopped at the first place we came to, and stayed in bed all the rest of the day. Tom didn't eat at all, and I finally tried that evening with a combination of half-ass Spanish and a smartphone to ask the girl at the bar if they had any cornflakes and milk. I figured I could stomach something simple like that. It took awhile, but she finally disappeared and came back with a package of some kind of chocolatey cocoa puffs kind of cereal. That didn't appear at all appetizing, so she disappeared again and this time came back with a brand new box of Honey Grahams, I think it was. Apparently, she had been grocery shopping at some point that day, and this was her husband's cereal. She sold me a bowlful for one euro, along with some room temperature milk. It was excellent. I hope her husband didn't mind.

I told Tom this story, and when I arrived later at his house in Coruna, he had bought me a huge box of cornflakes, along with bacon and eggs, which I had also mentioned beat the heck out of coffee and toast for breakfast every day. So I had cereal, bacon and eggs every morning while I was there.

We stay in touch, Skype once in awhile, and also talk on the phone. He is one of my dearest friends. Just the other night, my phone rang and it was an unidentified number. I answered, and it was Tom, calling at about 1 a.m. his time, and feeling pretty good after several glasses of his beloved brandy.

I asked Tom one time after our first Camino to tell me about his experience on the pilgrimage. It took him a long time to respond, as Tom is careful – and very good – with words. Here is what he wrote:

"You asked me to tell you about my Camino experience. Undoubtedly the single most marking five weeks of my life. I set out to basically prove to myself that I physically actually could do it. That was proven to be the case, and I can`t deny the satisfaction this has given me. But, however important that aspect was for getting me on my way, the really deep-felt and important consequences for me are very different. We were very lucky to have good weather and that was much appreciated, and thanks to Spain for that. The food was good but not great. The beer was very good and brings back fond memories. The brandy was almost enough to make the trip worthwhile, in itself. But, NO, for me and much to my surprise, the one aspect that made the experience unique and sacred were the people that providence had me meet and share time with. Each of those I met have given me important lessons:

"The Last Hippie: Paula, who goes through life without a fear in her mind. She lives quite happily not conforming to the rules and regulations which see the rest of us doing exactly what is expected of us, and obeying each and every social norm. I don't think she has ever held a job for more than three weeks, and is not in the least perturbed about not having the safety nets we all have, social benefits, insurance, pensions, medical health coverage, etc., etc. Whenever I feel that something IMPORTANT is going on, I ask myself what would Paula think about it all.

"The Last of the Vikings: Jytte, so full of energy she doesn't even have time to sleep at night. The prime example of Women's Liberation, in a country that leads the world in that aspect. Crane operator in a shipyard in her teens, i.e., the late '60s. She wanted to have a dog, she thought the dog would need to run around, so she went out and got herself a house with a garden. When lazy, I think of her and quickly get off my arse and start moving.

"Scaredy Cat: John, who thinks he's afraid of the world. So to put things in order, he gets on a plane, flies halfway round the world to a country with a language he doesn't speak, to walk for four weeks in the wild with no idea where he is going to be each night, with no telephone. To the rest of us, Texas Scaredy Cats come across as tigers. You were scared, so you went out and did something about it. Keep it up, John.

"The Northeners: Alf and Anita. Meeting them put me in touch with my early roots. They led me to think about Norway, and now I'll be going back to look for things I abandoned years ago.

"The Southerners: Enzo and Maria, showing and reminding us that the best thing in life is still to have someone to love and to show it. I actually felt a bit envious of them.

"I leave you with some considerations written by a famous author. The translation from Spanish is mine:

"With time, you realize that every experience shared with a person is unrepeatable. With time, you realize that the best was not the future, but rather the moment you were living in that instant. With time, you try to forgive or ask for forgiveness, say that you love, say that you miss, say that you need, say that you want to be a friend.

"All these things are understood with the passing of time. A friend once told me that we get old very soon, and wise too late. Just as one no longer has any time.

"Take care, old friend. Tom."

July 8

*T*oday, I was propositioned by two hookers in Madrid. Wow, pretty cool.

I'm not sure of the name of the street, but it's off Gran Via, which I'm guessing is basically Main Street. Along one stretch of it, among the outdoor cafes, tiendas, assorted other little stores and kiosks and things, are the sex shops and hookers. One of them actually followed me, "Where you from?" Then she grabbed my arm and tried to stop me, "Guapo, where you from? Guapo?" I just kinda smiled and shook my head and kept walking.

I screwed up my courage today and went exploring. With two days left until my flight home on Sunday, I knew I had to go check out the city. Not only would it be wasting a great opportunity, if I didn't, there's no way I could sit around the hotel all day without getting bored spitless, but I'd also be risking a dangerous bout of monkey brain syndrome. You know — me freaking out again about being 8,000 miles or whatever from home with no way to do anything about it.

So, I got on the Metro (subway) and hoped for the best. I admit, I was pretty nervous, but only I guess because it was something I'd never done before. I had my little subway map, with everything I needed to do circled and written down (the guy at the hotel told me basically what to do).

So I get to the subway station, go down the escalator and ... now what? Ain't nobody down there. No signs to speak of, or something —

anything – to indicate what I'm supposed to do next. Just a bunch of turnstiles and a row of ticket machines. Obviously, I need to buy a ticket and go through the turnstiles, but all the machines look different and what kind of ticket do I need? I try reading the information on the front of a couple of the ticket machines, but that's not helping. So I find a security hombre and he speaks a little English, but he's not understanding what I'm talking about. Finally, I whip out my little map and point to where I want to go. About that time, another hombre comes walking up, and shows me what to do. I've got my ticket (one euro) and I'm through the turnstiles and on my way.

And guess what? I made it to where I needed to go! I made it to Gran Via, got propositioned by Spanish hookers, found the Plaza del Sol and Plaza Mayor, bought a couple of souvenirs and ate some lunch ...

Somebody who read my blog asked why I thought it was cool to be propositioned by hookers. Well, it just was. Here I am, a guy from Texas who has never really been anywhere in the world, never lived anywhere besides Texas, and not only did I live for a month by myself in Spain and walk nearly all the way across the country with a backpack, I got propositioned by a couple of Spanish hookers in downtown Madrid! Wow – chalk that up to another experience I never would have imagined having.

Looking back now, I probably could have taken better advantage of the three days I was "stranded" in Madrid, but, heck, I think I did OK. After an all-night bus ride from Santiago de Compostela – which was pretty damn interesting, in itself – I arrived at Barajas airport about 7 a.m. My flight back home was three days away, but I was hoping they might be able to get me on an earlier plane. If not, I'd just have to wait it out.

It took a couple hours, but finally the Continental Airlines ticket office inside the airport opened, and the girl who worked there was really nice, and thankfully spoke English. She did her best to get me on an earlier plane, but in the end, there was nothing available. I thanked her, and headed for the area where you catch taxis and shuttle buses and other ground transportation.

I tell the guy at the information booth that I need a hotel room, and he makes a telephone call and says they are on their way to pick me up. Cool. I wait about five minutes, then start getting a little paranoid and a little impatient, so I walk outside and try to flag down my own ride to a hotel. I talk to two shuttle drivers, but apparently they are there to pick up people who already have a reservation at a particular hotel. I'm a little exasperated, but staying a whole lot calmer than I did when I first arrived and couldn't find a bus.

I head back inside to the information center, and my driver is standing there with the information guy. He tells me that rooms at his hotel are 55 euros per night. Sounds good, I say, and we walk out to his van. This guy is very nice but speaks absolutely no English. Nevertheless, we have a little hit-and-miss conversation as he takes me to the hotel, which is in a quiet little neighborhood near the airport.

It seems to be a nice enough place, but I ask the girl at the front counter if I can see the room. This evidently pisses her off. "It is not normal," she says, and takes me upstairs. The room is fine, and I ask if I can leave my backpack while we go back downstairs to register. "If you want to stay," she says, haughtily. "Yes, I do," I say, and lean my backpack against the wall.

As we are filling out a registration form, I tell her that I did not mean to make her angry by asking to see the room. I apologize, and she smiles and says it is OK. Evidently, she was offended by my request, but she accepted my apology and was fine after that.

So I hung out in Madrid for three days, navigating the subway system to go downtown and look around, see a few sights. Then it was time to go home.

A Small Favor to Ask

Thanks for reading this memoir; I hope you found this travelogue meaningful or helpful in some way. If you did, please take just a moment to write a brief review on Amazon. Your reviews mean a great deal to me and it helps my story reach others.

About the Author

 John Henry Clark is an award-winning journalist, freelance writer, author and avid golfer who was born and raised in Texas. He grew up in northwest Houston playing sports at Oaks Dads Club and attending church with his parents, but decided as he got older that things he learned in Sunday school no longer made much sense.

Since then, he has spent a lifetime seeking answers and exploring a variety of beliefs. After a successful career as a newspaper reporter, Clark turned his lifetime love for learning into a new career as a public school teacher, and that gave him time during the summer months to pursue his project to research and write a book describing what people believe about God and why they believe whatever it is they believe.

He crisscrossed his beloved state, interviewing fellow Texans at random, and uncovered dozens of fascinating, sometime gut-wrenching stories that reveal not only how life experiences, tragedies and triumphs can shape a person's view of the world and beyond, but also the commonalities shared by all people -- the desire for love and happiness. Read his book, *Finding God in Texas*, and find answers to the meaning of life, and maybe discover something new about yourself.

§ § §

Made in United States
North Haven, CT
19 May 2022

19343654R00095